SEP 1 4l

Life During
Medieval Times

Other titles in the *Living History* series include:

Living
HISTORY

Life During
Medieval Times

Toney Allman

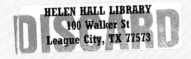

ReferencePoint
Press®

San Diego, CA

© 2014 ReferencePoint Press, Inc.
Printed in the United States

For more information, contact:
ReferencePoint Press, Inc.
PO Box 27779
San Diego, CA 92198
www. ReferencePointPress.com

LIBRARY OF CONGRESS CATALOGING-IN-PUBLICATION DATA

Allman, Toney.
  Life during medieval times / by Toney Allman.
    pages cm. -- (Living history series)
  Includes bibliographical references and index.
  ISBN-13: 978-1-60152-568-0 (hardback)
  ISBN-10: 1-60152-568-0 (hardback)
  1. Middle Ages--Juvenile literature. 2. Europe--Social life and customs--Juvenile literature.
  3. Civilization, Medieval--Juvenile literature. I. Title.
  CB351.A43 2014
  940.1--dc23
                                                              2013012394

Contents

Foreword

Hstory is a complex and multifaceted discipline that embraces many different areas of human activity. Given the expansive possibilities for the study of history, it is significant that since the advent of formal writing in the Ancient Near East over six thousand years ago, the contents of most nonfiction historical literature have been overwhelmingly limited to politics, religion, warfare, and diplomacy.

Beginning in the 1960s, however, the focus of many historical works experienced a substantive change worldwide. This change resulted from the efforts and influence of an ever-increasing number of progressive contemporary historians who were entering the halls of academia. This new breed of academician, soon accompanied by many popular writers, argued for a major revision of the study of history, one in which the past would be presented from the ground up. What this meant was that the needs, wants, and thinking of ordinary people should and would become an integral part of the human record. As British historian Mary Fulbrook wrote in her 2005 book, *The People's State: East German Society from Hitler to Honecker,* students should be able to view "history with the people put back in." This approach to understanding the lives and times of people of the past has come to be known as social history. According to contemporary social historians, national and international affairs should be viewed not only from the perspective of those empowered to create policy but also through the eyes of those over whom power is exercised.

The American historian and best-selling author, Louis "Studs" Terkel, was one of the pioneers in the field of social history. He is best remembered for his oral histories, which were firsthand accounts of everyday life drawn from the recollections of interviewees who lived during pivotal events or periods in history. Terkel's first book, *Division Street America* (published in 1967), focuses on urban living in and around Chicago and is a compilation of seventy interviews of immigrants and native-born Americans. It was followed by several other oral histories including *Hard Times* (the 1930s depression), *Working* (people's feelings about their jobs), and his 1985 Pulitzer Prize–winning *The Good War* (about life in America before, during, and after World War II).

In keeping with contemporary efforts to present history by people and about people, ReferencePoint's *Living History* series offers students a journey through recorded history as recounted by those who lived it. While modern sources such as those found in *The Good War* and on radio and TV interviews are readily available, those dating to earlier periods in history are scarcer and often more obscure the further back in time one investigates. These important primary sources are there nonetheless waiting to be discovered in literary formats such as posters, letters, and diaries, and in artifacts such as vases, coins, and tombstones. And they are also found in places as varied as ancient Mesopotamia, Charles Dickens's England, and Nazi concentration camps. The *Living History* series uncovers these and other available sources as they relate the "living history" of real people to their student readers.

Important Events in

476
The last Roman emperor, Romulus Augustulus, is dethroned.

1000
A century of invention in farming begins; devices such as the plow increase agricultural productivity and help double Europe's population.

1187
The Muslims under Saladin recapture Jerusalem from the Crusaders.

800
In Rome, Pope Leo III crowns Charlemagne emperor; his Carolingian dynasty rules Western Europe until 987.

1066
William of Normandy defeats the last Anglo-Saxon king at the Battle of Hastings, establishing Norman rule in England.

| 800 | 1030 | 1080 | 1130 | 1180 |

1189
Richard the Lionhearted becomes king of England and leads a failed attempt to reestablish Christian rule in Jerusalem.

732
A Christian army defeats Arabic forces in France, reversing the European advance of Islam.

1099
The First Crusade ends Muslim rule in Jerusalem.

632
The prophet Muhammad dies as Islam begins to expand both east and west of the Arabian Peninsula.

Medieval Times

1215
King John of England signs the Magna Carta, limiting the rights of the monarchy.

1347
The deadly bubonic plague strikes Europe and intermittently returns for the next 250 years.

1328
Charles IV dies, ending 341 years of successful rule by the Capetian kings who established modern France.

1378
The Great Schism, in which there are three claimants to the papacy, occurs.

1200   1250   1300   1350   1400

1294
Medieval Europe's greatest scientist, Roger Bacon, dies.

1431
Joan of Arc, one of France's patron saints, is accused of witchcraft and burned at the stake.

1337
The Hundred Years War begins between France and England.

1200
The rise of universities begins to promote a revival of learning throughout the West.

1453
Johannes Gutenberg prints his famous forty-two-line Bible at Mainz, Germany.

Introduction

The High Middle Ages

Medieval times are the historical period in Europe between the collapse of the Roman Empire and the birth of the era known as the Renaissance. The word *medieval* comes from the Latin term *medium aevum*, which means "middle age." The medieval era, therefore, is also known as the Middle Ages. The Middle Ages lasted approximately a thousand years and are generally divided into three eras. They are the early Middle Ages, stretching from about AD 476 to 1000; the high Middle Ages, occurring from about 1000 to the early 1300s; and the late Middle Ages, lasting until about 1500, when the Renaissance began. When people refer to medieval times, however, they often mean the period of the high Middle Ages.

Early, High, and Late Middle Ages

The early Middle Ages were a dark and dangerous time when it seemed that civilization and culture were lost. When the Roman Empire fell, the people of Europe slipped into a long period of disorder, strife, constant warfare, poverty, and intellectual stagnation. Cities disintegrated, and businesses and trade disappeared in a large part of Europe. Invaders plundered homes, farms, and villages. Epidemic diseases swept through populations. Different members of the aristocracy, or nobility, vied among themselves for power. Because of the misery and the loss of civilization and knowledge during this time, some historians have called this five-hundred-year period the Dark Ages.

Out of the suffering and chaos of the early Middle Ages, however, a new kind of organized civilization gradually emerged—one with kingdoms, renewed trade and commerce, towns and cities, and the unifying religion of Christianity in the form of the Catholic Church. This period of the Middle Ages was a time of relative prosperity and population growth. In a very real sense, it was the beginning of modern Europe. Historian C. Warren Hollister says, "In short, anyone who wonders how Europe was able to transform the world, for good or ill, into the global civilization that envelops us today must look to the medieval centuries for an important part of the answer. For during the Middle Ages, Europe grew from a primitive, rural society, thinly settled and impoverished, into a compelling civilization."[1]

Most of the growth of Western civilization occurred during the high Middle Ages, and this era is what most people think of as true medieval times. During the late Middle Ages, violence, warfare, and disease led to another period of disorder. The gains achieved during the high Middle Ages, however, did not disappear. Medieval society gradually changed again, and powerful European nations emerged under strong monarchies. The social and political organization of medieval Europe evolved into something new, but according to many historians, the medieval era was the foundation of modern Western civilization.

Medieval Society's Organization

Medieval times were dominated by the feudal system. Feudalism was a political and military system that organized and benefited the elite members of society—the nobility. Under feudalism, a king or overlord divided his lands into large tracts called fiefs and gave them to nobles, or lords, in return for promises of loyalty and military aid when needed. The noble became a vassal of the king or overlord; a vassal is a holder of land that is granted in return for obligations and promises of allegiance. In turn, each lord could parcel out some of the land to vassals of his own, who then owed loyalty and military service to the lord. A lord might be a member of the aristocracy or a church bishop or a pope, since the Church owned much

> **WORDS IN CONTEXT**
> **fiefs**
> The lands or estates granted to nobles.

Medieval Europe,
Circa 1250

NORWAY
SWEDEN
Stockholm
SCOTLAND
IRELAND
THE PALE
North Sea
DENMARK
Baltic Sea
LITHUANIA
RUSSIA
ENGLAND
WALES
Oxford
London
Amsterdam
FLANDERS
POLAND
Atlantic Ocean
English Channel
Paris
Mainz
Prague
Orléans
Holy Roman Empire
Vienna
FRANCE
NAVARRE
AQUITAINE
HUNGARY
Milan
PORTUGAL
Avignon
Bologna
Madrid
CASTILE
ARAGON
PROVENCE
PAPAL STATES
SERBIA
BULGARIA
Toledo
Rome
Granada
Naples
GRANADA
Mediterranean Sea
KINGDOM OF THE TWO SICILIES
Aegean Sea
AFRICA
SICILY
CONSTANTINOPLE
N

of the land in Europe. In the feudal system land, rather than money, determined wealth. Historians Frances Gies and Joseph Gies say that "feudalism united the European elite in a mutual-aid society."[2]

Concurrent with the mutual aid system of feudalism was the economic basis of society called the manorial system. The manorial system defined the relationship of the lord of the manor and the peasants, who were the vast majority of the people. "The manor" commonly referred to the lord's manor or castle plus one or more villages in the fief as well as the surrounding lands of the estate. Since the lord held the land, the peasants of the village worked for the lord in return for land of their own to work. The villages were under the control and protection of the lord, who basically provided the only government that the villages had. The people of the villages were divided into different classes of peasants. Some might be serfs who had few rights; others were considered free and owned their land, even though they were subject to the rule of the lord. The manorial system was a rigid hierarchy of classes of people who believed, for the most part, that their status was ordained by God.

As the High Middle Ages Progress

In the beginning of the high Middle Ages, people belonged to one of three classes: they were nobles, peasants, or clergy of the Church. The high Middle Ages, however, ushered in a period of great changes in Western civilization as people grew prosperous through social stability and advancing technology. By the time that the high Middle Ages drew to a close, the economy was based on money, not land. A new class of people developed, starting with early peddlers and traders, who eventually became a business class known as the burghers. These people, who established the towns from which cities grew, were independent of the lords and the manorial and feudal systems. They were the traders, businessmen, craftsmen, bankers, and manufacturers, as well as the common workers. From the high Middle Ages, modern Western European capitalism was born.

Whether in village, castle, or city, the lives of the people were dominated perpetually by the belief that they were a part of

> **WORDS IN CONTEXT**
> **manorial system**
> The social organization defining the relationship between a lord and the tenants of his estate who were obligated to work for the lord in return for use of the land.

Christendom, and the Church was a powerful influence on daily lives. This influence was both beneficial and corrupting. As the era evolved, the Church went from functioning almost as a government or state to embittering the public with its worldliness and greed. Nevertheless, Christian doctrine and spirituality determined much of the culture, morality, and intellectual growth of the high Middle Ages and was a critical civilizing force for all classes of people in society.

Chapter One

Castle Life

The castle was the place the lord lived and from which he ruled his fief, but the character of the castle changed as the high Middle Ages advanced and so did the lifestyle within the castle. At the height of the medieval era, the castle was a sumptuous residence that housed the lord's family, his knights, other dependents, and his servants. It was a center of elegance and graceful living.

The Development of Castles

During the early part of the high Middle Ages the lord's castle might be no more than a tall wooden tower, built for defense against invaders, whether foreign or from a neighboring fief. At that time the noble was, first and foremost, a military man and a warrior. His vassals were military men—knights—who followed him into battle. The knights helped the lord control his territory from the defensive tower. The lord, his knights, and his family did not live in the tower all the time; instead, it was used as a fortress during times of war from which to attack enemy raiders and warriors.

In the twelfth century the defensive towers began to be built of stone and to become dwelling places. They were still single towers, called keeps, which were perhaps two or three stories high, with a single room on each story. The lord and his knights lived in the tower, along with the lord's family, servants, and even guests. The keeps were dark, gloomy, crowded places. The windows were just small, high slits through which to shoot arrows. Everyone ate and lived in a single room and slept in a single bedchamber. In a cellar dug beneath the tower was the dungeon in which captured prisoners could be held or, more often, food supplies could be stored in case of a long siege by enemies. When a raiding party attacked the fief, any peasants who could escape ran to the keep for shelter, where they lived until the danger had passed. Sieges mounted by a neighboring lord who wanted to capture more land were common during this time. Historian Morris Bishop says that "sieges could often be very long, lasting as much as two years, and almost as exhausting to the besiegers as to the besieged."[3] The fighters in the keep were frequently successful in thwarting their attackers, but life inside a keep under siege was almost like life in a prison.

As the high Middle Ages progressed, raids and sieges became less common, the aristocracy grew wealthier, and architectural skills increased. The nobles wanted comfort and luxury as well as protection. Historian Raymond Ritter says, "By the late twelfth century the greatest feudal lords had just begun to discover how terribly sad, how poorly lighted and ventilated, were the dwellings in which family and servants lived crowded together in the most peculiar promiscuity."[4] By the thirteenth century large, elaborate concentric castles, or castle complexes, made their appearance in England. These complexes were surrounded by walls and moats and had drawbridges for defense. They included gate houses, courtyards, several attached buildings, and towers. The main tower was in the center of the complex and housed the lord and his family. Lords also resided in roomy, elaborate manor houses during the height of the medieval era. The manor houses were built for comfortable living, and if they were not always castles with towers, they might be fortified with moats or walls, and they offered the same kind of lifestyle as the castles. Castles and manor houses were the luxurious homes for the most powerful lords and kings, along with their families and vassals.

> **WORDS IN CONTEXT**
> **vassal**
> A noble under the protection of a lord, overlord, or king and subordinate to him.

Lord of the Castle

The great hall was the center of castle life. It was the large, public room where the lord demonstrated his authority, his power, his conspicuous consumption, and his value as a provider and protector. "Here," says

Bishop, "he held court, transacted affairs, entertained, and dined on trestle tables set up for each meal."[5]

At least two times a year, the English lord presided over the *hallmote*—the manorial court. The lord was responsible for enforcing criminal and civil law for all the people of the fief. In criminal cases, the defendant was tried by a jury of his or her peers, but the lord often decided guilt and penalty in civil complaints or who was correct when one person had a complaint against another. In 1307, for example, in the village of Elton, two vassals were involved in an argument. One claimed that the other had borrowed thirty-two pence from him and failed to repay it. Court records of the time show that the second man was ordered to pay the debt and was also fined an extra forty pence. Translated into modern English with standard spelling, the court document concludes, "And afterwards he came and made fine for 40 pence . . . and . . . he will be obedient henceforth to the lord and his neighbors."[6] Other recorded cases demonstrate the lord's understanding and generosity. Often the records show that a fine for misdeeds was forgiven because the defendant was too poor to pay it.

By the height of the medieval era the lord had become a courtly and bountiful gentleman, not a fighting man. He flaunted his wealth with lavish spending, especially on the food he ate and was able to provide for the people under his protection. In England the most important meal of the day was dinner, served at 10 a.m. to the lord, his family, his vassals, and any guests. One book of etiquette of the time explains, "It is not seemly that a lord should eat alone."[7] The lord sat at the head of his table. Other people, in order of status, sat at tables below the lord's table. Everyone dined on stews, roasts, white bread, pastries, cookies, and wine. In Italy the menu included pastas, rice dishes, nuts, and cheese, as well. The dinner might include several meat dishes, including beef, chicken, pork, starlings, peacocks, storks, and venison. When the long feast was over, servants with baskets collected leftover bread and bones and gave them to the poor waiting outside the door and the dogs that waited beside them.

WORDS IN CONTEXT

hallmote

The court of justice presided over by the lord of the manor.

The lavish lifestyle of the lord was admired by many but not everyone. In the late-eleventh century, a monk wrote about Hugh, the earl of Chester, in England, "Many honorable men, clerics, and knights were also in his entourage, and he cheerfully shared his wealth and labors with them. . . . He kept no check on what he gave or received. . . . A slave to gluttony, he

Lords of the medieval era flaunted their wealth by holding lavish banquets. At some of these banquets, entertainers (pictured) performed with songs, storytelling, juggling, or acrobatic stunts.

In Their Own Words

For the Love of War

Many medieval knights gloried in battle. Bertrand de Born was a French noble and troubadour who wrote poems and songs during the twelfth century. He celebrated the pleasures of war in many of his poems, such as the vivid example below:

My heart is filled with gladness when I see

Strong castles besieged, stockades broken and
　　overwhelmed,

Many vassals struck down,

Horses of the dead and wounded roving at random.

And when battle is joined, let all men of good lineage

Think of naught but the breaking of heads and arms,

For it is better to die than be vanquished and live. . . .

I tell you I have no such joy as when I hear the shout

"On! On!" from both sides and the neighing of
　　riderless steeds,

And groans of "Help me! Help me!"

And when I see both great and small

Fall in the ditches and on the grass

And see the dead transfixed by spear shafts!

Lords, mortgage your domains, castles, cities,

But never give up war!

Quoted in L. Kip Wheeler, "Cult of Chivalry," Dr. Wheeler's Website, Carson-Newman College. http://web.cn.edu.

staggered under a mountain of fat, scarcely able to move."[8] A lord could be greedy and a spendthrift, but by his generosity he maintained his status and influence and kept the loyalty and approval of the people under his rule. After the less elaborate supper in the evening, he also showed his bountifulness by the entertainment he provided for his household.

When they were available, the lord would invite entertainers into the castle hall. Bishop describes the entertainment, "After the evening meal the castle's population might assemble to watch a floor show, presented by traveling minstrels, jugglers, acrobats, or contortionists, and sometimes trained dogs or monkeys; or they might listen to a storyteller recalling high deeds of the past and faraway wonders. He would pause at thrilling moments to announce: 'Whoever wants to hear more must open his purse.'"[9]

Singing and music were popular, too. One of the songs from the thirteenth century goes, "Merry it is in halle to hear the harpe, The minstrelles synge the jogelours carpe."[10] (*Jogelours* are jongleurs, who were minstrels, poets, and entertainers. *Carpe* means to chatter and tell jokes.)

Other entertainments led by the lord might include chess, card games, gambling, and different sports such as hunting and tournaments. He also arranged fairs and holiday celebrations for the amusement of the whole estate. For the most part, however, the lord oversaw activities for his household, and it was usually a large one, including the lady, their children, the vassals and knights, and other relatives and guests.

> **WORDS IN CONTEXT**
> **keep**
> The inner stronghold of the castle or its main tower.

The Knights

The lord's knights were particularly likely to need diversion in times of peace because they were fighters and warriors who longed to honor God and their lord in battle. Knights willingly went on raids of neighboring fiefs to plunder and kill for the glory of the castle and to capture any wealth for their lord and themselves. In peacetime a good lord kept his knights busy honing their skills in military practice and sports. The activities helped keep the knights in line and prevented them from fighting among themselves. In the castle the knights began each day by training with their weapons and horses. One exercise was tilting at a *quintain*. The quintain was a post, often set up with a swinging sandbag. The knight rode full speed toward the quintain, tilting at it with a lance or spear. If the knight's thrust was not on target, the sandbag swung around and hit him as he rode past. Knights would also hold meetings among themselves to talk about battle strategies or how to defend against or conduct sieges.

In the afternoons knights often joined the lord in sports that increased their skills, such as hunting and falconry. Deer were the game most often hunted. In falconry, the gentlemen hunted birds and other small game with trained hawks. The most favored sport for knights, however, was the tournament. Tournaments were war games during the early part of the medieval era, and deadly serious. Bishop explains,

> Large parties gathered and divided into sides, usually on a territorial basis [by differing fiefs]. At a signal from the herald they charged with leveled lances. Those who were brought down continued to fight on foot. Any sort of stratagem was permitted; the defeated could be pursued into the open country and captured. Once a knight yielded, he . . . surrendered his horse and armor or a suitable money ransom. Squires [young apprentice knights] dragged out the fallen, who were likely to be numerous. In one enormous tournament near Cologne [in Germany] more than sixty knights were killed.[11]

By the end of the twelfth century, tournaments became more like festivals with demonstrations and contests and feats of skill. Knights fought with heavier armor for protection, blunted swords and lances, and under specific rules. People came to watch, and ladies cheered for their favorite knights and awarded prizes to the winners. Knights became more gentlemanly and were regarded more as nobles themselves than as brutal

WORDS IN CONTEXT

quintain

A post with a sandbag attached used by knights for tilting exercises.

With his lance extended, a knight rides toward a quintain built to look like a soldier holding a shield (lower left). During peacetime, knights often engaged in such activities to hone their fighting and riding skills.

warriors. They followed a code of chivalry, a moral code of conduct that described proper behavior both in war and toward their society. Chivalric knights aspired to be brave, honorable, courtly toward women, faithful to God and his Church, and gallant and kind to the weak and the poor. Although no formal, written code of chivalry existed during the high Middle Ages, many accounts of knightly qualities appeared in poems and songs, and the aristocrats of later times wrote about medieval chivalry and its code of virtues. In the fifteenth century, the Duke of Burgundy listed the twelve knightly virtues. They were: "Faith, Charity, Justice, Sagacity, Prudence, Temperance, Resolution, Truth, Liberality, Diligence, Hope and Valour."[12]

One aspect of chivalry was the concept of "courtly love." Courtly love was the idea that ladies should be loved and wooed with grace and romance. A knight might compose love songs or poems for his lady or defend her honor in a duel or offer her small gifts as love tokens. He never, however, married her. When knights did marry, they were usually given land and manors of their own by the lord, but noble marriages were not for love. Marriages were alliances between aristocratic houses, and as one writer of the time, Andreas Capellanus, advises, "Everybody knows that love can have no place between husband and wife."[13] A knight's courtly love was by definition a romance with an unavailable, already married woman whom he honored and loved from afar. Perhaps she was his lord's lady.

The Lady

Every lord of the castle or manor had to have a lady because having children, continuing his line, and establishing an heir to the estate was of utmost importance. Marriages were arranged—often in infancy—by noble families in order to help them increase their wealth and influence. Women had no choice about whom they married and were subject to their husbands in all things. Nevertheless, the lady of the castle was not without power. She was responsible for managing the household, overseeing the servants, and caring for the young children. She also could legally own property and manage or sell it. When the lord was away from the castle—perhaps at war— she managed the estate, kept the accounting books, and made the decisions about ruling the fief. Sometimes, the lady might have all the control in the castle. If her husband was old and senile or sick or weak, she could take charge. A monk of the time wrote of a lady known as Avicia countess of Evreux, "The count of Evreux's intellect was by nature somewhat feeble as well as being blunted by age. And putting perhaps undue trust in his wife's ability, he left the government of his county entirely in her hands."[14]

Usually, however, the lady of the castle engaged in more traditionally feminine activities. Her daily schedule was similar to the lord's. She began her day by being dressed by her servants in one of her expensive, elegant, brightly colored gowns. Her choice of gowns was important because her dress reflected her status. She wore or carried embroidered gloves that were decorated with jewels. Servants also helped her arrange her elaborate hairstyle, perhaps in braids or extravagant coils. Most important was the headdress, or hair decorations. The lady might wear gold

Looking Back

Chivalry for Equals Only

Chivalry had a particular meaning for the medieval knight that does not necessarily fit with modern ideas about honor and fairness. Knights in battle were especially likely to apply the chivalric code only to their own kind. Historian Richard Abels explains:

> Fighting "fairly" is a modern misconception of chivalry. Medieval warfare . . . was characterized by pillaging and ravaging; it was directed against civilian populations. . . . Chivalry dictated, for example, that quarter be given to defeated knights. Once a captured knight had given his word (parole), he would be released on the promise that he would pay the agreed upon ransom. On the other hand, foot soldiers were killed as a matter of course, and ambush and maneuver were considered consistent with chivalry, as was the massacre of the civilian populations of towns that were taken by storm.

Richard Abels, "Medieval Chivalry," United States Naval Academy. www.usna.edu.

dust sprinkled over her hair or a gold net or circlet of precious metal. Some could afford coronets and tiaras decorated with pearls or gemstones. Preparing for the day took a long time.

The lady joined her lord for meals and afterward might participate in hunting if she wished or watch a tournament. If she had a favored knight in the contests, she might give him one of her gloves to carry into the mock battle as a token of courtly love. Other leisure activities included embroidery, dancing practice, and, if she was educated, reading and writing poetry. Some castles had a room by the kitchen where ladies could bathe together in a social group. In the evenings ladies often joined the men in games such as blind man's bluff or ring-around-a-rosy. They might have "torch dances," in which each dancer carried a candle and tried to keep it away from all the other dancers, who were trying to blow it out.

The Children

Despite all the choices in entertainment, much of a lady's day was devoted to her duties toward her children. Large families were common in medieval times, and women were responsible for the early education and care of both boys and girls. Even in the castle, life for children could be dangerous in medieval times. Often the lady's minimal knowledge of herbs, first aid, and hygiene were the only resources available should medical care be needed. Diseases and accidents took many lives, and the mortality rate for children was high. Some historians estimate that close to 50 percent of children died before the age of ten. Eleanor of Aquitaine, for example, gave birth to eleven children and survived all but two. The risk of losing children, however, did not make parents love them less, and families grieved for lost children. One father, Giovanni di Pagolo Morelli of Florence, writes about the death of his son Alberto, "Months have passed since his death, but neither I nor his mother can forget him. His image is constantly before our eyes, reminding us of all his ways and habits, his words and gestures. . . . For more than a year, I have not been able to enter his room, for no reason other than my extreme grief."[15]

Servants serve food to a medieval lady and her guests. The lady's choice of gown and headdress let others know her status.

No matter how many children survived in the castle family, they were usually pampered and indulged. They had toys such as dolls (called "poppets") made of cloth or wood, small metal figures of horses and knights, jumping jacks, child-sized bows and arrows, blocks, rocking horses, tops, and pinwheels. They played games such as checkers and ball games similar to handball and bowling. In addition to play, children were given tasks to do. They made up beds and ran errands for the lady of the castle. They learned their letters and prayers from her, as well as good manners, such as how to be polite at the table.

By about the age of seven, the lives of boys and girls began to take different paths. Girls were kept separated from boys in their own bed-chambers to protect their innocence and purity. As they grew older, boys were often sent away to another castle to become pages. There, they began their training as future gentlemen and knights under the tutelage of the male household members. They learned dancing, chess, and elegant serving at the dinner table, as well as tilting with lances, fencing with blunted swords, and hunting. Girls might be sent to a religious school run by nuns or to another castle where they learned to be fine ladies. They might practice embroidery, weaving, music, and dancing. The lady of the castle taught the girls along with her own children. They learned to manage the household, keep financial books, cook, sew, handle the servants, or choose the right wine for dinner. Both boys and girls were commonly educated in reading, literature, and in Latin (the language in which most books were written). Usually, girls were taught at home by tutors or priests. Boys might be sent away to school or have tutors at the castle.

The Family Line Continues

All of the young people living in the castle were the responsibility of the lord and lady. As their own children grew up, the lord and lady settled their futures with suitable marriages, careers, gifts of land, and manors of their own. The pages became squires at the age of fourteen, and after seven years, they could become noble knights. The girls returned home, and their futures were settled by their families. With the right marriage, the young woman became the elegant lady of a castle herself and established a family of her own.

Chapter Two

Village Life

Under the manorial system village life was very different from castle life. Peasants worked hard, lived poorly, and faced many hardships. In the early high Middle Ages, peasants struggled just to survive, but as the centuries passed, many peasant families were able to achieve a relatively prosperous life. In a typical English village, there might have been three kinds of peasants. The most comfortable were the free peasants. They held their own land and were free to sell it and move away and to make decisions for their children in important matters such as marriages and careers. The serfs did not own their land but belonged to it. They were subject to the lord's will in almost everything and owed him a percentage of everything they grew or acquired, as rent for their homes and the land they worked. The cotters were the poorest of the peasants; they had no land and lived by working for the lord and other peasants. All the peasants paid for the protection of the lord and the use of his land by working the lord's demesne. The demesne was the tract of land attached to the manor. It belonged to the lord as did anything grown on it, but the peasants had to work it. Basically, the whole village was dominated and owned by the lord of the manor or castle.

> **WORDS IN CONTEXT**
> **cotter**
> A poor serf who had little or no land to work.

Village Organization

A typical village might include about three to six hundred peasants. They lived in a central cluster of homes divided by dirt lanes and surrounded by their fields. Often the agricultural land was divided into three different fields, so that the farmers could practice crop rotation. This meant that each field was plowed and planted only once every three years. The land was held individually, but the villagers made community decisions about which field to plant, when to sow seeds or harvest crops, or when farm animals would be allowed to graze in idle fields. The fields of the village were usually bounded by forest, river, or meadowlands. These areas belonged to the lord but commonly could be used by the villagers with the lord's permission. The lord's manor or castle might be in the area if the lord held just one village, but if a lord ruled several villages, his manor might be quite a distance away.

The ordinary English village consisted of the peasants' homes, a church, a community well for water, a community water mill where grain could be ground, and a community oven where villagers could bake their bread. The village was a crowded and busy place. Frances Gies and Joseph Gies say,

> The village scarcely presented the tidy appearance of a modern English village. Houses did not necessarily face the street, but might stand at odd angles, with a fence or embankment fronting on the street. The nexus [center] of a working agricultural system, the village was a place of bustle, clutter, smells, disrepair, and dust, or in much of the year mud. It was far from silent. Sermons [from medieval times] mention many village sounds: the squeal of cartwheels, the crying of babies, the bawling of hogs being butchered, the shouts of peddler and tinker, the ringing of church bells, the hissing of geese, the thwack of the flail at threshing time. To these one might add the voices of the villagers, the rooster's crow, the dog's bark, and other animal sounds, the clop of cart horses, the ring of the smith's hammer, and the splash of the miller's great waterwheel.[16]

The Village Dwellings

Each family in the village had its own dwelling. A few of the cottages might be large, such as those of free peasants, but some were just the tiny

A typical medieval village (similar to the view in this fifteenth-century woodcut) usually included houses for peasants as well as a communal water well, mill, and oven. Most villages were dusty, noisy, smelly places.

huts or hovels of the cotters. Most of the homes were much alike. They were built with timber frames, and the walls were made by a procedure called wattle and daub. Wattles are upright wooden stakes driven into the ground. They are woven with tree twigs and branches. Then, the whole

In Their Own Words

"I Am Not Free"

Around the year 1000, an English writer authored an imagined conversation between a lord and a serf. The dialogue demonstrates the burdens of the peasant's life at the time. The lord is given the title "master" and the serf is called "ploughman" (plowman):

Master. What sayest thou ploughman? How do you do your work? *Ploughman.* O my lord, I work very hard; I go out at dawn, driving the cattle to the field and I yoke them to the plow. Nor is the weather so bad in winter that I dare to stay at home, for fear of my lord: but when the oxen are yoked, and the ploughshare [cutting blade] and coulter [front, groundbreaking spike] attached to the plough, I must plough one whole field a day, or more. *Master.* Have any assistant? *Ploughman.* I have a boy to drive the oxen with a goad, and he too is hoarse with cold and shouting. *Master.* What more do you do in a day? *Ploughman.* Certainly I do more. I must fill the manger of the oxen with hay, and water them and carry out the dung. *Master.* Indeed, that is a great labor. *Ploughman.* Even so, it is a great labor for I am not free.

Quoted in Herbert Applebaum, *The Concept of Work: Ancient, Medieval, and Modern.* Albany, NY: SUNY Press, 1992, pp. 223–24.

structure is daubed or smeared with mud, clay, and manure. The roof was thatched with whatever material was available—straw, marsh reeds, heather, or perhaps the leaves of water plants called rushes. Thatched roofs were cheap and easy to make, but they had to be repaired and replaced frequently. They were homes to mice, rats, birds, spiders, and insects of all sorts. Floors were just dirt, sometimes covered with straw that vermin also infested regularly, and there were no chimneys or fireplaces. Peasants cooked at a central hearth of stones and let the smoke rise to a small hole in the ceiling. Homes were often dark and smoky. Small window openings, if there were any, were covered with wooden shutters at night and during the winter.

A small yard, called a toft, was in the front of the peasant's house, and animals often grazed there. The larger croft (perhaps half an acre) was at the rear of the house where a vegetable garden could be grown and any animals that the peasant owned could be penned. The most prosperous peasants might also have a manure pile in the croft for fertilizing their gardens. Animal waste was valuable, but people's wastes were a problem. They did not have outhouses or privies in their yards. Sometimes they dug a small trench in the yard, but usually, report Gies and Gies, they handled elimination needs simply by "retiring to 'a bowshot from the house.'"[17] This meant the distance an arrow could be shot from a bow—far enough away to avoid fouling the immediate environment and to get a little privacy. For toilet paper, they used moss, grass, or hay.

> **WORDS IN CONTEXT**
> **toft**
> The yard of a villager's cottage.

The Peasant Couple

Inside the peasant house life was simple and basic, with few luxuries. Most houses held nuclear families (husband, wife, and children), but sometimes old people or other relatives shared the home. Unlike the nobility, the peasant husband and wife usually knew each other before marriage because they were from the same village or a neighboring village. They chose each other (with parental permission) and were often bonded by love or friendship. Peasant society frowned on loveless marriages that were arranged for money or property. In 1303 an English monk wrote that it was a sin to marry a woman "for love of her cattle." He penned in verse (translated into modern English):

When it is gone and all is bare
Then is the wedding sorrow and care.
Love and cattle then are away,
And "wellaway" they cry and say.[18]

The peasant couple exchanged vows in the Church, and, if the couple were serfs, the father of the bride paid a fee called *merchet* to the lord of the estate for the marriage. The bride also brought a dowry—a gift of land, money, or personal goods—to the marriage. If the father of the groom was a prosperous free man, he gave a gift of land to the young man to help him get established. When the couple had no assets, they married without paying merchet, without dowries or gifts and without anyone's permission. Historian Eleanor Searle explains, "Free marriage was the prerogative of the foolish and the penniless."[19]

Family Life in the Cottage

The peasant couple occupied a cottage that might be only one room or might have a partition to separate the sleeping area from the living area. A large home might have three rooms, but the third was usually a *byre*, or stable, for the farm animals. Peasants with one room brought the animals inside the house at night for protection, and all slept together. When the children were born the whole family slept together in one room, with parents perhaps in a bed and the children on straw mats on the floor. A typical peasant family had few furnishings other than a bed. They had a trestle table with stools for eating meals, perhaps a trunk for holding valuables, and the household and farm tools needed for survival.

Bread is prepared for baking and a hog is being bled for butchering in a medieval village. The diet of peasants consisted mainly of black bread, beans, peas, turnips, cabbage, and ale. Meat was generally served only for special occasions.

Morris Bishop says, "The housewife had her domestic equipment—fine irons, a pot hanger, iron pots and a skillet, a cauldron, a washtub, bowls, jugs, baskets, a besom [broom], perhaps a cheese press and a kneading trough [for making bread]. The husband owned his tools—hoe, spade,

Looking Back

The Medieval Agricultural Revolution and Prosperity

From the beginning of the high Middle Ages until its peak in the early fourteenth century, the population of Europe more than doubled. This growth was made possible by an agricultural revolution that produced abundant food for the estimated 80 million people living in Europe by about 1300. Historian C. Warren Hollister explains:

> The heavy plow, drawn by a team of oxen, was the machine most crucial to high-medieval agriculture, but horses were important as well. They were of enormously greater significance in the High Middle Ages than in Roman times because the new horse collar allowed them to pull loads with their shoulders instead of their necks. Additional energy was supplied by tens of thousands of water mills and, later, by windmills. The new agriculture produced food in greater abundance and greater variety than before: protein-rich peas and beans became for the first time an important element in the European diet, and there was greater consumption of cheese and eggs, fish and meat.
>
> Consequently, Europe's population was not only much larger in 1300 than in 1050 but probably healthier, too, and more energetic.

C. Warren Hollister, *Medieval Europe: A Short History, Fifth Edition*. New York: Wiley, 1982, p. 148.

axe, scythe, knife, shears, whetstone, a yoke for carrying buckets. With only a few differences, his possessions were those of a poor American frontiersman not so long ago."[20]

When crops grew well and harvests were good the peasant family ate well enough, but the fare was simple. Peasants survived on black bread, pottage (soups and stews), vegetables from the garden, such as beans, peas, onions, turnips, and cabbage, and ale. Meat was for special occasions and usually it was pork from butchering one of the peasant's lean, wild hogs that ran free and foraged in the surrounding forest. Prosperous peasant families might also have eggs, cheese, and porridge. In some ways the peasants' diets were better than those of the nobility: Peasants ate whole grains and vegetables instead of the meat-heavy diet of the aristocracy, who also scorned vegetables. The upper class prided itself on avoiding peasant food and believed that what the peasants ate was suited to peasants alone. One poet of the aristocracy wrote, "Why should villeins [serfs] eat beef, or any dainty food? Nettles, reeds, briars, peashells are good enough for them."[21]

Little is known of the intimate family life of peasants because they were illiterate and left no records of their lives. Some clues about them come from written records such as court cases, coroner's reports of deaths, and religious sermons and commentary. Modern historians do know that peasant families usually had fewer children than noble families. In the fourteenth century Bishop Alvarus Pelagius wrote disapprovingly about peasant husbands who "often abstain from knowing their own wives lest children should be born, fearing that they could not bring up so many, under pretext of poverty."[22] The children that were born into the family, however, were loved and valued no matter how poor the family.

Growing Up in a Peasant Family

Babies were born at home with a midwife's help. They were baptized immediately in case they died. When a priest was not available, whoever was present performed the simple ceremony. If they survived infancy, small children were allowed to play as their parents worked. As children grew older, they did farm and household chores, and by the time they were teens, they joined in the adult work. They did not go to school. Children made up their own games and invented their own toys. Sermons of the time describe children using sticks, stones, and flowers to build pretend houses or sailing a piece of stale bread in the river as a boat. Using their imaginations, children were reported to have ridden long sticks for horses and to have made swords out of stiff reed stalks.

The lives of children, and even of adults, were precarious because the incidence of disease and accidents was high and no medical care was available. People suffered with fevers, skin boils, diarrhea, and stomach troubles for which they had no explanation and no cures. They faced contagious diseases such as smallpox, measles, typhus, leprosy, and even bubonic plague. Doctors were unavailable to the peasants, and even if they had been, they would have done little good. The doctors of the time knew nothing of germs or effective treatments. Famine was occasionally a danger, too, and children were most at risk of death during these times. In 1125 in England, for example, an old English Journal reports, "In this same year was so great a flood on Saint Lawrence's-day [in August], that many towns and men were overwhelmed, and bridges broken down, and corn and meadows spoiled withal, and famine and pestilence . . . in men and cattle, and in all fruits such unseasonableness as was not known for many years before."[23]

Fatal accidents, however, commonly affected more children than famines did. Historian Barbara A. Hanawalt has researched coroners' reports of accidental deaths of children during the fourteenth century. Of the coroner's reports she studied, Hanawalt found that 33 percent of the infants who died were killed in their cradles because of house fires. Most often the infants were left unattended while the parents were working outside. Fires in peasant houses were common, and the straw and thatch burned quickly if set off by a spark from a cooking fire. Older children suffered accidents such as drownings, falls, and mishaps with dangerous tools. Hanawalt describes some of these accidents: "For instance, a two-year-old girl tried to stir a pot of hot water but tipped it over on herself. . . . One three-year-old boy was following his father to the mill and drowned; another was watching his father cut wood when the ax blade came off the handle and struck him."[24]

Peasants plow and sow seeds in a field located just outside of the town gates. Payment to the lord for the use of his land usually consisted of a portion of grain or other crops or sometimes a certain number of eggs from the peasant's chickens.

A Life of Hard Work

Children's activities often mirrored the activities of their parents, and adults lived lives of almost constant hard work and physical labor. Women worked in and around the home. They did the cooking, cleaning, gardening, child care, weaving of cloth, and caring for any farm animals. They carried home water from the wells and washed clothes, and when necessary they joined their husbands in field work. Men plowed, planted, cultivated, and harvested their crops—sometimes by hand but, if they were lucky, with the help of a team of oxen. With the lord's permission the family gathered wood from the forest or fished in his river. Hunting in the lord's forest was not allowed. Poaching the lord's hunting lands was considered a serious crime, and a peasant might be killed or have a hand cut off for breaking this law.

From everything the peasant grew or acquired, he owed the lord a percentage or a fee in addition to the rent he paid for the use of the land. Often the peasant had no money, so he paid in kind—in the goods he had, such as a portion of grain or a certain number of eggs. In addition, each peasant owed the lord a set number of days per week working the lord's demesne. A prosperous free peasant might pay a cotter to take over this obligation, but everyone else had to ensure the lord got his crops. The unceasing farming work was difficult, especially for the serfs, who could barely harvest enough of their own crops to survive.

> **WORDS IN CONTEXT**
> **demesne**
> The land attached to the manor that was retained by the lord for his own use and benefit.

For everyone in the village, life was complicated by the lord's constant demands for fees and fines. Peasants had to pay a fee to use the lord's mill to grind their grain and to use his ovens to bake their bread. They paid a fee to get married and a fee when a father died and his son or widow took over the land. They paid fines for failing to pay rents on their houses or failing to hand over the proper number of eggs from laying geese or for not participating in haying the lord's fields. They even were fined for failing to keep their sheep in the lord's barn during the winter so that the lord could have the manure for his own fields. In the village of Elton, in

1320, four peasants were fined "threepence" each for letting too many bean seeds fall into each hole during planting time. This was, according to village court records, "to the damage of the lord."[25]

Despite the burdens he placed on the village in order to enrich himself, the lord sometimes could be generous, if only to ensure the peasants' cooperation. At haying time, for instance, a lord was expected to provide a feast for the workers, and the feast had to be elaborate and to include meat. Haying was one of the most burdensome and miserable jobs, and the feast encouraged peasants to show up for the work. The lord also usually waived fines for poor peasants who could not afford to pay for their small transgressions. Cotters were excused from plowing duties on the lord's demesne because they were too poor to own plows.

Holidays Make Life Bearable

The lord respected holidays, too, and granted relief from work for the whole village during these times. At least once during every season of the year, the village observed a holiday. Peasants celebrated Christmas, Easter, May Day, harvest festivals, and some other holy days, such as Candlemas in February and All Hallows' Eve. The holidays were welcome days off from labor. Villagers celebrated with bonfires, dancing, singing, drinking, and sporting games, such as wrestling, ball games, rooster fights, and archery contests. They held pancake suppers and sometimes staged plays in which people dressed up as members of the opposite gender and acted silly. On May Day they might have decorated their homes with green, leafy branches and flowers, erected a maypole for dancing, and crowned a queen of the May.

The Christmas holiday lasted twelve days. During that festival a good lord provided a magnificent feast for the village. Some lords invited the peasants into their great halls for the feast. Others gave them only the leftovers from the meats of their own feasts. For example, if the lord's feast included a butchered deer, he gave to the peasants the parts he did not want for himself. They were called "umbles" or "numbles," meaning entrails, and typically included the heart, liver, tongue, feet, and brains. British educator Jane Gilbert describes one noble feast in

England to which just two peasants were invited—a prosperous one and a poor one:

> The first got a feast for himself and two friends, including beer, beef and bacon, chicken stew, cheese—and even candles to light the feast with. The poorer peasant did not fare so well. He had to bring his own cup and plate. But at least he got to take home the leftovers, and he was even given a loaf of bread to share with his neighbours. This was used to play a traditional Christmas game: A bean was hidden in the loaf, and the person who found it became king of the feast.[26]

Generous, wealthier lords also might give small gifts, including pennies for the poorest peasants. Other lords required peasant guests to provide the firewood and then provided them with a meal of bread, soup, and meat. After dinner the peasants were allowed to sit around in the hall drinking beer.

Breaking the Grip of Serfdom

Holidays broke up the bleak, hardworking existence that peasants had to endure, but for most serfs and cotters, life could be full of misery and hunger much of the time. As the high Middle Ages advanced and towns and cities grew, many peasants bought their freedom or just ran away to look for a better life. By law in medieval Europe, any serf who was able to live in a town for a year and a day without being caught by the lord was granted freedom. In the high Middle Ages, people said, "Town air brings freedom."[27] The growing towns and cities welcomed village refugees, and they created new classes of medieval people.

Chapter Three

City Life

As the high Middle Ages progressed, cities grew. The traders and peddlers of earlier times became the artisans and businessmen who formed cities. These people often became wealthy, and at the same time, they helped the nobility who sponsored and protected them become wealthier, too. The city entrepreneurs formed a new social class—the burghers or bourgeoisie. In turn, they created a new class—the working class, who were hired to perform all the labor required in the city. The working-class people might not have been much better off than serfs and cotters in terms of what they owned or how they lived, but they were free to make their own way in the world.

> **WORDS IN CONTEXT**
> **burgher**
> A middle-class or prosperous, solid citizen of a town or city.

The Structure of the City

By modern standards, medieval cities were small. Information about city populations is limited, but it has been estimated that London, for example, had a population of between 30,000 and 35,000 in the twelfth and thirteenth centuries. By 1300, in all of Europe there were perhaps fifteen cities with populations of 50,000 or more. In Italy, Florence had a population of approximately 100,000 and Venice had a population between 85,000 and 100,000. The French city of Paris may have been the largest European city in the high Middle Ages, with population estimates between 80,000 and 200,000. Even though cities were not large, however, they were crowded, bustling, noisy, dirty, and sometimes dangerous.

All kinds of people lived crammed together in the cities, including businessmen; craftspeople such as shoemakers, tailors, and carpenters;

shopkeepers; day laborers; wealthy merchants and bankers; religious leaders; city officials; runaway serfs; and criminals. Some lived and worked in splendid stone homes and buildings, but most houses and structures were built like those in peasant villages, with thatched roofs and wattle and daub walls. These structures were crowded right up against the narrow streets—often two or three stories tall and narrow, but with the upper story overhanging the street.

The buildings were so close together that rapidly spreading fire was a constant danger. In 1221 the mayor of London enacted a law requiring that houses be constructed with slate or wood shingle roofs, but many in the city ignored the law because thatch was so cheap. In Vienna a similar law assessed a large fine against the family who owned the house where a fire first started. Nevertheless, fires wiped out whole neighborhoods regularly during medieval times. In the twelfth century, William Fitzstephen, a London clerk and author, wrote of his beloved city, "Among the noble cities of the world that Fame celebrates, the City of London of the Kingdom of the English, is the one seat that pours out its fame more widely, sends to farther lands its wealth and trade, lifts its head higher than the rest. . . . The only pests of London are the immoderate drinking of fools and the frequency of fires."[28]

The City's Environment

Fitzstephen praised London as a beautiful, healthy, happy city. He described its magnificent structures, such as its castles, the Tower of London, its cathedrals, and the mansions of the wealthiest townsmen. He wrote of London as glorious and noble, but London was also a place with a murder rate twenty times that of modern-day London. C. Warren Hollister says, "The violence of medieval London may be attributable in part to the existence (in 1309) of 354 taverns and more than 1300 ale shops."[29]

Every medieval city was a rough, rowdy place, but apparently some were worse than others. Paris, for example, has been described as orderly

The Italian city of Venice (pictured in this page from a fifteenth-century illuminated manuscript) was one of the larger cities of medieval Europe. Most cities of the time were crowded, noisy, dirty, and sometimes dangerous.

(by medieval standards), with many paved streets, a police force, and even an effort at garbage collection. One French merchant was appalled by his visit to London. He said it was full of "degenerates" and wrote of gambling dens, theaters with "belly dancers" and shameless singing and dancing girls, and crowds of beggars and crooks in the streets. He advised, "Every evil or malicious thing that can be found anywhere on earth you will find in that one city. . . . So if you don't want to deal with evildoers, don't go to London."[30]

London is a good example of the typical busy, dirty city environment of the high Middle Ages. Most people spent their days outside, and every imaginable activity took place in the streets. Morris Bishop says,

> The medieval streets were unquestionably foul. Butchers slaughtered animals at their shop fronts and let the blood run into the gutters. Poulterers flung chicken heads and feathers into the streets. Dyers released noisome [smelly] waters from their vats. City officials in Italy would throw the fishmonger's unsold fish into the street for the poor, to make sure it would not sicken honest purchasers. Pigs ran free as scavengers, and in London "genteel dogs," though not commoners' dogs, were allowed to roam at will. Flies settled in clouds to their banquets. . . . The walker, perhaps with a perfumed handkerchief to his nose, picked his way carefully, dodging the black mud thrown up by the squash of horses' hooves.[31]

Few cities had a sewer system, either, and no one had a bathroom, so sanitation was a serious problem. A story is told of King Louis IX, who was made a saint after his death in 1270. "Once," relates historian William R. Enger,

> he and his men rode through the narrow streets of Paris, early in the morning to avoid later crowds. Now, buildings reached right to the street, and upper stories actually extended out over the street. In such rooms there was a trapdoor in the floor so that the chamber pot might be conveniently emptied out into the street below. That morning, the king of France was showered by the contents of a chamber pot, and he ran to the house to get the rascal. When Saint Louis found out that the culprit was a student who had risen early to do his lessons, he gave him a scholarship instead.[32]

People were supposed to shout "Look out below!" when they dumped their waste or garbage into the streets. Then, anyone on the street had to duck and jump out of the way as fast as possible.

Middle-Class Burghers

Kings, as well as people from all walks of life, had to cope with the dirt and noise of the city, and for the emergent middle class—the burghers—it was worth it. Most burghers were of the middle class. They were bakers, butchers, tavern owners, artisans, and craftsmen. In order to protect themselves and their standard of living, most craftspeople and artisans belonged to guilds. Guilds were like the trade unions of today. Merchants had guilds to protect their interests, lobby the city government for favorable laws and treatment, and to maintain monopolies. Craft guilds protected the artisans' wages or the amount he could charge for his goods, set up training rules for apprentices, and set quality control standards for the goods produced. Membership in the guild was restricted, and that made an artisan's quality product (such as a knife handle) more valuable, which helped the craftsperson earn enough to maintain a middle-class income.

> **WORDS IN CONTEXT**
> **poulterer**
> A merchant who deals in poultry, hares, and game.

Middle-class burghers usually lived in two- or three-story houses. The street level room was the workshop or store (sometimes both), and the upper stories were the single room levels where the family lived. The kitchen would be at the rear of the building on the ground floor. The entire family slept in one room up the narrow stairs and used the third level (if they had one) for a living and dining area. The furnishings of the dwelling were often as simple as in a peasant house. The family had a table and benches or stools, one or more chests for valuables, a bed for the parents, and a cupboard and shelves for dishes, tools, and miscellaneous property. When they could afford it, the family might imitate the noble class by decorating the home with wall hangings of embroidered cloth or tapestries. They might also have a screen that could be used to section off an area of the main room during an occasional bath taken in a small tub. All the family participated in the business. Wives, sons, and daughters learned the trade or craft by watching and practicing the skills of the trade. Although women were subject to their fathers and husbands, widows often took over the business and ran it successfully when their husbands died.

The Rich Burghers

Wealthier burghers, who were merchants, manufacturers, bankers, lawyers, and government officials, lived crowded lives, too; but their homes imitated the layout of castles by including a great hall and one or more bedchambers for sleeping. These burghers built actual fireplaces and brick chimneys for warmth in the hall and for cooking. If a family had servants, they carried the day's water supplies from the river or from city wells, cooked the meals, and slept in the kitchen or with the children. Well-off burgher families also had privies of a sort. These were outside and discharged by means of a gutter into a cesspit at the rear

of the house. Periodically, workers were hired to clean out the cesspit and haul the contents away.

For their time, burghers lived very well and comfortably. In many ways they imitated the lives of the nobility, for whom they often felt both envy of their status and scorn for their pretensions. Wealthy burghers could buy whatever the nobles could and sometimes more. They ate all the food they wanted in wide variety. They wore the latest clothing fashions. They could acquire exotic spices and fruits from faraway places, jewels, and luxurious home decorations such as carpets and silks. They had leisure time, and no one to tell them what to do with it. An anonymous French poet of the early fourteenth century writes, "To be a free burgess [burgher] is to be in the best estate of all; they live in a noble manner, wearing lordly garments, having falcons and sparrow-hawks, fine palfreys [riding horses] and fine chargers [war horses]. When the vassals are obliged to join the host [answer the lord's summons], the burgesses rest in their beds; when the vassals go to be massacred in battle, the burgesses go to picnic by the river."[33]

The sons of the burghers attended some of the first secular or non-religious schools, where they studied commercially useful subjects such as arithmetic and languages instead of Latin and philosophy.

Like bakers and craftsmen, butchers represented the burghers, or emerging middle class, of medieval times. Burghers usually lived in two- or three-story houses, often above their businesses.

In Their Own Words

One View of City Life

Francesco Petrarch was a fourteenth century scholar and poet who lived for years in the city of Avignon, in France. Petrarch hated the city and gives a vivid description of the worst of its characteristics. The complaint appears in one of his books of letters, written to the saint in history that he most admired, Saint Augustine. In the passage below, he imagines telling Saint Augustine about Avignon:

> I am fatigued beyond all expression, with this noisy, dirty city; it is the gulf of all nastiness and vice: a collection of narrow, ill built streets, where one cannot take a single step without meeting with filthy pigs; barking dogs; chariots which stun one with the rattling of their wheels; sets of horses in caparison [harness], which block up the way; disfigured beggars, terrible to look at; strange faces from all the countries upon earth; insolent nobles, drunk with pleasure and debauch; and an unruly populace, always quarreling and fighting.

Susanna Dawson Dobson and Jacques François Paul Aldonce de Sade, *The Life of Petrarch*. Philadelphia: Samuel A. Mitchell & Horace Ames, 1817, p. 152. http://books.google.com.

Girls were sometimes sent to religious schools run by nuns, the same schools that noble children attended. Middle-class boys were also sent to a craftsman or artisan as apprentices to learn a trade. The children of prosperous peasants, seeking a better life, might become apprentices, too. Bishop explains, "The apprentice was bound for a term of years to a master, who engaged to teach him the trade's mysteries, to treat him as a good father would, to tend to his spiritual and moral welfare, to beat him to his benefit. At the end of his term he took an examination and became a journeyman."[34] Journeymen then spent another few years wandering to different towns and working for other craftsmen until, after a final examination by the guild, they qualified as master craftsmen themselves. Middle-class girls occasionally became apprentices in the clothing trade, but usually they married and participated in the husband's trade.

The children of wealthy burghers lived more leisurely lives than those of the middle class, although they were expected to perform household chores. These young people were educated to be genteel ladies and gentlemen like the aristocracy. Nevertheless, a father would never send his sons away to be pages, like sons of the nobility, or to live as apprentices. The wealthy burgher wanted his sons to remain at home and learn to take over the business someday. Daughters, especially in the cities of Italy, were given rich dowries and often married poor members of the nobility so that the family could have aristocratic ties. Noble families might have looked down on the burghers as bourgeois, but the nobility envied and wanted their wealth.

City Fun and Games

Like the people in the countryside, residents of the cities enjoyed entertainments and sports. City people of all ages loved games, perhaps more than country people did since they got little of the physical activity in their work that peasants had. Almost all medieval cities had playing fields for sports, as well as areas in the city at times given over to watching plays and pageants or engaging in games. Fitzstephen found much of London's entertainment praiseworthy. For instance, he writes,

> Let us begin with boys' games (for we were all boys once). Each year on the day called "Carnival" schoolboys bring fighting-cocks to their schoolmaster, and the entire morning is given over to the boyish sport, for there is a school holiday for purpose of the cock fights.

After lunch all the youth of the city go out into the fields to take part in a ball game. The students of each school have their own ball; the workers from each city craft are also carrying their balls. Older citizens, fathers, and wealthy citizens come on horseback to watch their juniors competing, and to relive their own youth vicariously: you can see their inner passions aroused as they watch the action and get caught up in the fun being had by the carefree adolescents.[35]

People held all sorts of contests for fun. They engaged in wrestling, archery and javelin contests, horseracing, sword fighting, foot racing, and more cruel sports, such as bull, boar, and bear baiting. Baiting games involved setting attack dogs on a chained or penned wild animal and letting them fight to the death. An even gorier game was sometimes popular in Italy. It was called the evil cat game. Bishop explains, "A man bare to the waist, with his head shaved, entered a cage with a cat and tried to kill the cat with his teeth, without using his hands or losing his eyes."[36] During the Middle Ages cats were regarded as evil and associated with witchcraft and the devil. Superstitious people saw nothing wrong with killing cats, but, even at that time, some more educated and religious people disdained this barbaric sport.

More carefree and gentler games could be played in winter. Adults and children alike enjoyed snowball fights, and sliding on the ice was popular, too. Fitzstephen adds, "Others are more skilled at frolicking on the ice: they equip each of their feet with an animal's shin-bone, attaching it to the underside of their footwear; using hand-held poles reinforced with metal tips, which they periodically thrust against the ice, they propel themselves along as swiftly as a bird in flight or a bolt shot from a crossbow."[37]

Townspeople enjoy themselves at a medieval archery festival. Archers' guilds, in what is now Belgium, regularly held such festivals, which often included archery contests, performances by jesters and musicians, and a feast.

Looking Back

Middle-Class Marriage and Partnership

Unlike the nobility, who married for aristocratic ties and expansion of wealth and influence, the bourgeoisie of the cities often incorporated concepts of partnership, cooperation, and affection in their marriages. Middle-class couples depended on each other. Historian Harald Kleinschmidt explains:

> In the fourteenth century, it became customary among merchants to write private letters. Through these letters, merchants would communicate with their wives while they were on business journeys. It was not uncommon to include declarations of love and expressions of care into these letters. The presence in these letters of a tone of affection shows that, contrary to the aristocracy, the "bourgeois" families took it for granted that the married couple should be united in love. The integration of emotionality into "bourgeois" married life may have been due to the fact that the residents of the urban communities of towns and cities usually arrived as uprooted persons who had cut the ties to or were disinherited by their extended kin groups in the rural countryside. Hence these newly immigrating settlers were induced to develop novel families from scratch which could be based on new principles of household organization. . . . Because "bourgeois" families could only thrive if they succeeded in competing with rival merchants and artisans within the same and among different towns and cities, the mutual cooperativeness of the family members was essential to the continuing existence of the family.

Harald Kleinschmidt, *Understanding the Middle Ages: The Transformation of Ideas and Attitudes in the Medieval World.* Rochester, NY: Boydell, 2000, p. 138.

The Working Class in the City

City people of every class enjoyed entertainments, but for the poorer working classes, to own luxuries, such as balls or fighting dogs or horses or even ski poles, was not possible. Instead, these people at the bottom of city society could participate freely in games like snowball fights. They watched the plays put on for the public outdoors. For the most part, however, historians believe that in most circumstances the working class had little to make life comfortable or enjoyable. The common workers in the city came from every different class of feudal society. They could be escaped serfs, perhaps criminals, maybe the younger sons of poor nobility who would inherit nothing. They might be alcoholics who had been members of the nobility or free peasants who had lost everything to their addiction. They could be former soldiers and knights who had no land or money or apprentices who had failed to learn their craft. Some had been disabled by accidents or disease; some were family members left destitute by a father's death. All these people might be drawn to the city in the hope of making a living.

People of the working classes were the unskilled laborers of the city. They might do odd jobs that no one else wanted to do, such as collecting sewage, sweeping the streets, perhaps acting as porters when a heavy load had to be moved from one place to another, or unloading trade ships when they arrived in port. Luckier ones could be servants for wealthy burghers. Others might work for people who owned clothing and textile businesses. They did not work in factories (which did not yet exist) but in their own small homes. They received the raw materials for their work from the manufacturer or merchant who handed it out from his place of business. They took the materials home, performed the labor required, returned the finished product in the specified amount of time, and were paid extremely low wages for their efforts. This kind of industry is called piecework or the "putting-out system." Textiles expert Krystal Morgan describes an example of piecework:

> Typically, a weaver-draper would purchase wool from a wool merchant on credit. The wool would be delivered to the weaver-draper's home workshop, where his employees (mostly female)

sorted, washed and greased the wool. The wool was then "put out" to a succession of domestic workers—carders or combers, spinners of fluffy warp and tightly twisted weft yarns, warpers and weft winders, all mostly female, mostly earning piece-work wages. Weavers, dyers and fullers were more likely to be male. The weavers might be employed by the weaver-draper, or work in their own homes. Finally, the weaver-draper would sell the finished goods to a cloth merchant, and pay the wool merchant from his profits.[38]

Some of the lowest classes survived only by charity as beggars, and others turned to lives of robbery and crime. The poor of the city were usually ignored unless they caused trouble. Bishop says, "They were free, of course, but free only to look for work, honest or dishonest, and to go forever hungry and cold."[39]

Remembering the Poor

Little is known about the daily lives of the poor people at the bottom of medieval society. Almost no one of the time wrote about their lives, and they were illiterate and left no records of themselves. Historians do know that wealthy burghers sometimes worried about being right with God and, therefore, being kind to the poor. The Church taught that the poor were the ones who would be blessed in heaven, while the rich were in danger of going to hell. In their wills rich burghers often left instructions that any debts owed them by poor people should be forgiven. To save their souls, most wealthy people gave regular donations to the Church and also left large donations in their wills. At every level of society, in the city and in the countryside, the Church and religion were ever-present components of daily life and thought.

Chapter Four

Religious Life

The Catholic Church was the great unifying force in Western Europe during the high Middle Ages. Religion made people feel that they belonged to a larger group—not a nation or a monarchy but the union of Christendom. The Church wielded great political and spiritual power and tied together everyone in western Europe's Christian world. During the medieval era the Church established its organization, or hierarchy; it laid out the sacraments that ordered people's lives and ensured them a place in heaven; it detailed the morality and responsibilities that people owed to God. For people of the Middle Ages religion dictated behavior, and religious activities were central to day-to-day living. The Middle Ages was an age of faith.

> **WORDS IN CONTEXT**
> **Christendom**
> The Christian world of Europe.

The Church Hierarchy

In the Church, the pope was recognized as God's representative on Earth, and he appointed the cardinals—the high clergy of the Church. The cardinals, guided by prayer and God, elected a new pope from one of their own when the pope died. The pope was the head of the Church, very much like a king. The cardinals were his court, who assisted him at his palace. Under the cardinals were the bishops—the lords of the Church. The bishops ruled local areas in the countryside, towns, and cities. They lived like nobles and often controlled their own lands and villages. Lowest in the hierarchy were the village priests, who answered to the bishop. These priests were often minimally educated and as poor as a free peasant, but they still commanded utmost respect from the people.

The whole hierarchy of the Church believed that it had the right to rule society and demand obedience to its teachings.

Monks, friars, and nuns were an important part of the Church, too, but outside the hierarchy. The pope and his representatives claimed authority over the monks, friars, and nuns, but in practice these people sometimes went their own ways. Monks were people who joined monasteries to devote their lives to God, religious learning, and prayer, often rejecting worldly activities. Friars devoted their lives to God, too, but usually by taking vows of poverty and living in the world of everyday people, where they could strive to help others. They often wandered from village to village, preaching to the people and living by begging. Friars spurned the monks as being more devoted to themselves than to caring for others. Nuns were women who joined convents and lived separated from the world, as did the monks. Monks and nuns were supposed to renounce worldly things and devote their lives to God, but sometimes they seemed to give up only marriage and to enjoy many earthly comforts.

In the Monastery or Convent

Despite their devotion to God and prayer, monasteries and convents did have contact with the rest of society. Monks in monasteries taught the sons of the nobility. Some peasant boys attended monastic schools, too, in order to learn basic reading, arithmetic, and Latin. Sometimes, the younger sons of the nobles (who would not inherit the estate) or of free peasants were given to the monasteries as children, trained and educated, and then ordained as monks themselves when they grew up. Girls of the nobility might be sent to convent schools, where they were given a basic education in reading and were taught skills such as sewing and embroidery.

Daily life in some monasteries and convents could be austere and based on self-denial, but in others life could be quite pleasant. Many monasteries and convents were wealthy. Historian Christopher Holdsworth explains, "So the monastery or convent was an attractive place for material, as well as spiritual reasons, and especially so to those who

In Their Own Words

The Peril of Sacrilege

Pagan Peverel was a knight who had participated in the first Crusade. He came home to England and then seized by force two villages belonging to the Ramsey Abbey monastery. The monastery sued and got back its property. The incident did not end there however. Saint Ivo, the patron of Ramsey Abbey, took earthly and miraculous revenge on Peverel for daring to cheat the Church, as well as on two other men who had the misfortune of being associated with the knight. According to a biographer of the time:

"On that same day [that the court ruled against Peverel], before Pagan arrived at his lodging, the horse on which he was riding had its feet slip from under it and fell three times to the ground . . . and a hawk which he was holding was shaken from his hand and made for the wood in swift flight, never to return. The horse of the priest who was travelling with him slipped and fell as well, and its neck being broken— although the priest was unharmed—it breathed its last. There was also Pagan's steward, called Robert, who came in for a more deserved punishment [in the form of a severe illness], because ... most faithful to his master, he had given his approval and assistance to the man's wickedness."

Quoted in Frances Gies and Joseph Gies, *Life in a Medieval Village*. New York: Harper & Row, 1990, p. 29.

lacked a secure place in the world—to younger sons without a patrimony [inheritance], or to daughters who preferred the safety of virginity to the perils of childbirth and the tedium of child rearing."[40]

Women chose a life in a convent for different reasons. Most were of the upper classes, and in many convents nuns did not really renounce the

A medieval couple brings their son to a monastery, as depicted in this thirteenth-century illustration. The younger sons of nobles or of free peasants were sometimes given to monasteries to be trained, educated, and eventually ordained as monks.

world. They had much leisure time, wore elegant clothing and jewelry, kept pets, were allowed to sing and dance, could own private property, and could go on vacations. Some women were forced into the convent by their fathers, perhaps because they had no money for a dowry for a good marriage, perhaps because they were handicapped in some way that made them unmarriageable, or occasionally to get them out of the way in a family dispute over power and rule. The Clio Project—an organization devoted to women's history—reports that one woman of the time complained, "I was not good enough for man, and so am given to God."[41] Most nuns in convents, however, chose their calling. Some were intellectual women who wanted a quiet life of study. Others were deeply religious. Many found a convent a happier, freer place to live than the nonreligious world. A medieval writer compares the life of a wife versus that of a nun with this advice:

> And how I ask, though it may seem odious, how does the wife stand who when she comes in hears her child scream, sees the cat stealing food, and the hound at the hide? Her cake is burning on the stone hearth, her calf is sucking the milk, the earthen pot is overflowing into the fire. Though it be an odious tale, it ought, maiden, to deter thee more strongly from marriage, for it does not seem easy to her who has tried it. Though, happy maiden, who hast fully removed thyself out of that servitude as a free daughter of God and as His Son's spouse, needest not suffer anything of the kind."[42]

Church Doctrine for Everyone

Even though life in a monastery or convent was not all prayer and serving God, most of the members were devoted to their calling. Both in the religious community and in the secular world, God, the devil, heaven, and hell were very real and meaningful parts of day-to-day life. The Church—in the person of the priest, the bishop, the pope, or the head of the monastery or convent—laid out the required path to God and morality and told people what they must do to please God. Everyone tithed to the Church. This meant that they gave ten percent of all they earned or acquired to the Church. If they did not, they risked losing the path to salvation.

Everyone was also expected to make the seven sacraments a meaningful part of their lives if they wanted to be right with God. The first sacrament was baptism, and without it, no soul could be in the presence of God after death. Confirmation was the sacrament through which an older child or teen confirmed his or her commitment to the Church and God. Marriage was a sacrament, and Holy Orders was the sacrament by which a man chose "marriage" to the Church as a priest. Extreme unction (last rites) was the blessing and forgiveness performed for a sick or dying person by a priest. Penance was the act of confessing and being forgiven for one's sins. It was a sacrament that would be repeated over and over throughout a person's life, as was the sacrament of Holy Communion. Communion is the sacrament of receiving the body and blood of Christ, in imitation of Jesus's Last Supper, in the form of bread and wine blessed by the priest. Hollister explains, "The sacramental system, which only assumed final form in the High Middle Ages, was a source of comfort and reassurance: it made communion with God not merely the elusive goal of a few mystics but the periodic experience of all believers. And, of course, it established the Church as the essential intermediary between God and humanity."[43]

Crusades for God

The Church's influence was so powerful that its pronouncements affected not only spiritual lives but also political decisions. The pope's words were law. It was because of Pope Urban II, for example, that the Crusades were launched. The Crusades were a series of military expeditions undertaken by Christian Europe during the Middle Ages to seize the Holy Land (where Jesus had lived) from the Muslims. Christendom viewed the Muslims as infidels and, therefore, enemies of the true religion.

In 1095 Urban II gave a speech calling for Christians to wrest the Holy Land—especially Jerusalem—from the Muslims, or Saracens, as they were then known. In his speech the pope urged people to "go to defend the house of Israel." He said any fighters who did so would be avenging the mistreated Christians who lived in the Holy Land as well as God himself. He raised a cross before the audience and cried, "It is Jesus Christ Himself who leaves His Sepulcher and presents to you His Cross.

At the pope's urging, nobles, knights, and peasants alike joined in the Crusades, which began in 1095. Crusaders, such as the knights pictured here, traveled to the Holy Land in hopes of seizing it from the Muslims.

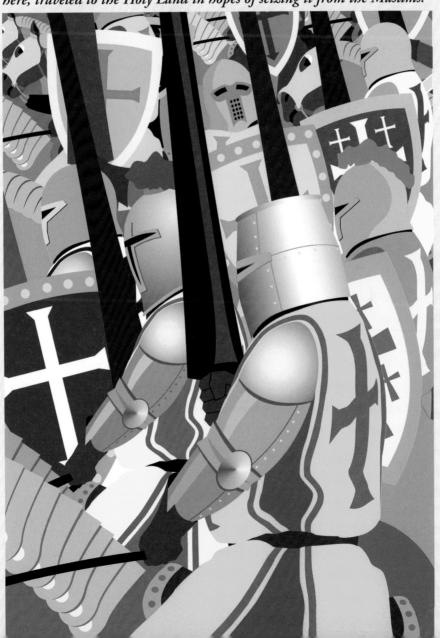

It will be the sign that will unite the dispersed children of Israel. Raise it to your shoulders and place it on your chests. Let it shine on your arms and banners. Let it be for you the reward of victory or the palm of martyrdom. It will be an unceasing reminder that Our Lord died for us and we should die for Him." The assembled people jumped to their feet and shouted, "God desires it! God desires it!"[44]

All across Christendom thousands of people—knights, nobles, and peasants—responded immediately to the pope's call. They marched with zeal to fight against the Saracens in the Holy Land and laid siege to the walls of Jerusalem. A French priest, Fulcher of Chartres, participated and later wrote an account of the battle. He writes, "At length our leaders decided to beleaguer the city with siege machines, so that we might enter and worship the Saviour at the Holy Sepulchre. They constructed wooden towers and many other siege machines." He goes on to describe a determined assault on the city's walls that went on "day and night" for three days, with counterattacks from the defending Saracens and many deaths, until finally the attackers succeeded. He reports, "One of our knights, named Lethold, clambered up the wall of the city, and no sooner had he ascended than the defenders fled from the walls and through the city. Our men followed, killing and slaying even to the Temple of Solomon, where the slaughter was so great that our men waded in blood up to their ankles."[45]

The Crusaders were cruelly violent and bloodthirsty. Another eyewitness, Raymond of Agiles, writes of the capture of Jerusalem:

Some of our men cut off the heads of their enemies; others shot them with arrows, so that they fell from the towers; others tortured them longer by casting them into the flames. Piles of heads, hands and feet were to be seen in the streets of the city. It was necessary to pick one's way over the bodies of men and horses. But these were small matters compared to what happened at the temple of Solomon, a place where religious services were ordinarily chanted. What happened there? If I tell the truth, it will

Looking Back

The Jews in Christendom

Many Jewish people lived throughout Christendom during the high Middle Ages. Many had peaceful, prosperous lives, but they were usually treated as second-class citizens. With the onset of the Crusades, this prejudice grew into a kind of crazed violence by some Christians against Jews, even though the Church issued edicts declaring that Jews should be protected as God's chosen people. Historian C. Warren Hollister explains:

Well might a twelfth-century Jewish merchant be unenthusiastic about urban life in England—or for that matter, throughout much of Western Christendom. For in a civilization that was almost unanimously Christian, members of a minority faith were apt to suffer. In most regions of Christian Europe, Jews had long been subjected to legal disabilities and popular bias. And their condition worsened in the High Middle Ages with the growth of Christian self-awareness, militancy, and popular devotion to the suffering Christ. Good Christian theology insists that Christ died for the sins of all humanity, but popular sentiment often held that he was murdered by the Jews. And there were those who arrived at the grotesque conclusion that the "murder" should be avenged. The persecution of Jews—and of other dissenting groups such as heretics and magicians—represents the wormy underside of high medieval Christian piety.

Quoted in C. Warren Hollister, *Medieval Europe: A Short History*, 5th ed. New York: Wiley, 1982, p. 159.

exceed your powers of belief. So let it suffice to say this much at least, that in the temple and portico of Solomon, men rode in blood up to their knees and bridle reins.[46]

The Crusaders were not able to hold the Holy Land permanently. The Saracens retook Jerusalem as time passed. Several more crusades followed, infused with religious fervor, but they were never successful. In the end, the Christian Crusades were a financial and military disaster that caused the deaths of many thousands of people to no purpose.

Gaining Heaven's Blessings: Saints and Relics

Despite the failures of the Crusades, the disasters and bloodshed were far away from the ordinary lives of most people of Christendom. For almost everyone, the Church and unwavering religious belief remained ever present in their daily lives. People in all walks of life strove to live their lives by the sacraments and accepted Church doctrine as truth. Families said morning and evening prayers and blessings before meals. They attended mass on Sundays and Christian holidays. People prayed not only to God and Christ, but also to the Virgin Mary and to the saints. The saints were people who were recognized by the Church as having lived holy lives, credited with one or more miracles, and certain to have already entered heaven. Most people, according to the Church, did not go to heaven immediately upon their deaths; they spent time in Purgatory, atoning for their sins. Saints had attained heaven, and unlike God, who was a stern, implacable judge, saints were kind and forgiving and would intercede with God to help a person on Earth. People believed saints could heal them, protect them, defeat their enemies, and drive away the devil.

Unlike the educated intellectuals, most common people combined religion with a kind of mystical superstition. People believed that God and the saints would bless and help them if they had magic tokens or made pilgrimages or acquired relics. Charms might be holy images, small crosses, or holy pictures. The clergy and educated people might see these objects as reminders and representations of their religion, but common people often thought they would ward off evil. Relics were the physical remains of a holy person or saint or something that had touched them. For example, a piece of clothing that had been worn by Jesus or the Virgin Mary, a piece of the cross on which Jesus was crucified, or a vial of blood from Jesus were most holy relics with great power. Relics of saints might include a piece of bone, a lock of hair, a tooth, or a preserved drop of sweat. Many people believed relics could heal disease and injury or at least bring one closer to God. Some churches maintained collections of relics in shrines.

> **WORDS IN CONTEXT**
> **pilgrimage**
> A journey to a sacred place.

During the medieval era, historians say, there was a cult of relics. Relics were so important that bodies of saintly people were treasured. Thomas Aquinas, for example, a much-loved priest, philosopher, and gentle religious scholar, died while visiting the monastery of Fossanova in Italy in 1274. The monks of the monastery were sure that Aquinas would be declared a saint by the Church, and they felt greatly honored and blessed that Aquinas had given himself to the monastery by dying there. The monks buried him at the monastery, but they then began to fear that they would lose his body—their cherished relic. A medieval Church inquiry that was considering Aquinas's sainthood reports,

> About eight months later there came a rumour that the Dominican Peter of Tarentaise had been made pope and that he wished the body of brother Thomas transferred to one of the greater churches of his Order. So the monks of Fossanova, fearing to lose the body, selected three of their number who dug it up one night and cut off the head, which they hid in a secret place in a corner of a chapel behind the choir. . . . The monks argued that if they had to lose the body, they might at least keep the head.[47]

Later, when the monks did not lose the body after all, they boiled it all to remove the flesh and preserve the bones as relics.

Only the very wealthy or high Church officials could afford to own a relic personally, but anyone could decide to make a pilgrimage to a shrine to visit a relic. Such pilgrimages were very popular during the high Middle Ages. The pilgrim was blessed at his church before he began his journey, and he wore a special robe and carried a staff. Usually, he traveled with a group of other pilgrims. Morris Bishop says, "A pilgrimage could be very gay. On entering a town a party formed ranks behind a bagpiper and marched through the streets, to the applause of bystanders. All sang and rang their little bells, which in England were called Canterbury bells. . . . Along the road they sang hymns and holy songs, and told each other stories."[48]

On the Dark Side

Religion could bring joy to medieval people, but it was a source of fear, too. The devil was always wandering the world, searching for people to be his victims. God was always ready to punish those who strayed from His path. Educated and uneducated people alike believed in witches who had made a pact with the devil or his demons and could curse other people. The supposed witches were tortured, tried, and put to death for their crimes. In the Church, preachers attempted to frighten people into goodness with terrible tales of suffering in hell. One preacher in England, for example, graphically described the miseries of men in hell. He said, "If one of them would give a thousand pounds for one drop of water, he gets none. . . . There shall be flies that bite their flesh, and their clothing shall be worms. . . . And in short, there are all manner of torments in all the five senses, and above all the pain of damnation: pain of privation of the bliss of heaven, which is the pain of all pains."[49]

The Church got rich on people's fear of damnation. Donations to the Church meant promises of time off in Purgatory and God's forgiveness for sins, which could be bestowed only by the priest. Wealthy people could even buy freedom from church rules, such as fasting during the

The Rouen Cathedral rises in the background of this street scene in the French town of Rouen. Wealthy residents paid for the tower's construction and in return received permission from the Church to eat butter during Lent.

pre-Easter period of Lent. At the Rouen Cathedral in France, for example, a new tower was built with money given by rich people who thereby received permission to eat butter during Lent. Even today, it is nicknamed the Butter Tower.

For the Good of the People

Corruption was a part of religious life in medieval times, but the Church had its good and truly Christian side, too. It established the first hospitals, poorhouses, and orphanages. Its law was that the poor were to receive a quarter of the tithes given in every village and one-half of all other Church donations. Monks and nuns ran many hospitals and refuges, such as the Hôtel-Dieu in Paris. It was established on the principle of charity and love for the poor. Historian Ellen N. La Motte explains, "No distinctions were made as to social standing, nationality or religion; the only condition necessary for admission was that the applicant show 'the signs of poverty or of misery,' upon which he was received and welcomed, and the order given to treat him 'like the master of the house.' To all who thus asked it the Church extended freely a simple and noble hospitality."[50]

Many members of the clergy were humble, loving people who tried their best to help others. These people of the Church were also the repository of education and literacy, and they passed on their knowledge as teachers and writers. Without the Church's influence, the intellectual life that began to flourish in the high Middle Ages would not have been possible.

Chapter Five

Life of Learning

As the high Middle Ages advanced and people prospered, an interest in philosophy, logic, science, and literature began to flourish. Intellectual curiosity and scholarly pursuits became an acceptable part of western European culture for everyone who had the means to seek an education.

The Medieval University

Beginning in the twelfth century, universities were established. Some of the first were the University of Salerno and the University of Bologna in Italy, the University of Paris, and Oxford University in England. These universities were under the control of the Church, but usually they were run independent of Church law. They managed this independence by avoiding the control of local bishops and declaring themselves allied with the pope. The pope was often more liberal about acceptable teachings, and he was also farther away and less likely to interfere with the curriculum. This stratagem meant that universities could offer studies in nonreligious areas of philosophical thought, literature, and science, along with more traditional religious instruction. A few secular schools were established at the height of the high Middle Ages as well.

> **WORDS IN CONTEXT**
> *trivium*
> The curriculum of learning consisting of grammar, logic, and rhetoric.

Northern universities such as Oxford and the University of Paris offered a liberal arts curriculum. The goal was a well-rounded, literate student body educated in philosophy and religious thought, or theology. The courses were based on the ancient Roman educational system. They included seven liberal arts, divided into the *trivium* and the *quadrivium*.

The trivium included three areas of study called grammar (organizing facts into reality), logic (understanding the facts), and rhetoric (the art of communication). The trivium studies taught students how to think. German academic Oliver Weis explains, "Sacred texts often refer to these 3 elements as knowledge, understanding and wisdom."[51] The trivium was the most important part of the academic curriculum. After its courses were mastered, liberal arts students moved on to the four parts of the quadrivium. It included arithmetic, geometry, music, and astronomy (which was much like astrology, also practiced at that time).

University curricula in southern Europe, such as in Italy and southern France, concentrated not so much on liberal arts as on medicine and law. They prepared students for careers, although they taught some liberal arts, too. At Bologna in Italy, law was the area of concentration. Historian Isabelle de Foix says, "The school at Bologna always had a practical nature; not for them the abstract theorizing of the nature of God that was done in Paris." The law curriculum at Bologna was an effort to create a just and reasonable system of law at a time when an organized legal system was rare in Europe. The system taught students to see "the law of the state as a mirror image of the rationality of the laws of nature."[52] Philosophy, religion, and practical knowledge were tied together during medieval times in a way that is not accepted today. Medicine, for instance, was often taught along with an emphasis on astrology and how the stars affect human health, while the need for just laws was linked to God and religion.

Student Life

Students at medieval universities might come from all parts of western Europe, and boys and men attended universities throughout Europe. At the University of Salerno in Italy, women were also allowed to attend. Entrance requirements varied with universities, but usually students were generally accepted from the nobility, the burgher class, or the free peasant class. Age was not a consideration either. The renowned Italian scholar and poet, Francesco Petrarch, for example, entered the University of Montpellier at the age of twelve. Most students, however, began

Scholars attend a lecture at the University of Paris, founded during medieval times. Universities of the period were controlled by the Church but functioned independent of Church laws. This allowed them to offer courses in philosophy, literature, and science as well as in religion.

In Their Own Words

How to Be a Good Medieval Doctor

At the Salerno medical school, a text titled "The Coming of a Physician to His Patient, or An Instruction for the Physician Himself," written by a physician named Archimattheas, gave practical advice for doctors. One sample reads:

> When the doctor enters the dwelling, of his patient, he should not appear haughty, nor covetous, but should greet with kindly, modest demeanor those who are present, and then seating himself near the sick man accept the drink which is offered him and praise in a few words the beauty of the neighborhood, the situation of the house, and the well-known generosity of the family—if it should seem to him suitable to do so. The patient should be put at his ease before the examination begins and his pulse should be felt deliberately and carefully. The fingers should be kept on the pulse at least until the hundredth beat in order to judge its kind and character; the friends standing round will be all the more impressed because of the delay and the physician's words will be received with just that much more attention. . . . When the doctor quits the patient he should promise him that he will get quite well again, but he should inform his friends that he is very ill; in this way, if a cure is affected, the fame of the doctor will be so much the greater, but if the patient dies people will say that the doctor had foreseen the fatal issue.

Quoted in James Joseph Walsh, *Old-Time Makers of Medicine.* New York: Fordham University Press, 1911, pp. 160–61. http://books.google.com.

their studies between the ages of fifteen and seventeen. Universities had no dormitories or cafeterias, and financial aid was not even considered. Typically, students lived in boarding houses or roomed in a home in the city that was close to classes. In a few universities, especially in Paris, wealthy patrons paid the room and board for poor students, but for the majority of students, going to the university was a financial hardship. At Oxford, the university provided a form letter to demonstrate how students should ask their parents or guardians for money. Translated from its original Latin, it reads:

> This is to inform you that I am studying at Oxford with great diligence, but the matter of money stands greatly in the way of my promotion, as it is now two months since I spent the last of what you sent me. The city is expensive and makes many demands; I have to rent lodgings, buy necessaries, and provide for many other things which I cannot now specify. Wherefore I respectfully beg your paternity that by the promptings of divine pity you may assist me, so that I may be able to complete what I have well begun.[53]

Finances were not a university student's only problem. The typical school day was long and rigorous. In Paris, for example, the day began at five or six o'clock in the morning. Students, summoned to classes by the ringing of the bells at Notre Dame Cathedral, converged onto the streets to make their way to the various lecture halls. There they sat on wooden benches or on the floor to listen to the professor lecture. The lecture might continue for hours, and students took notes on wax tablets. These tablets were wood covered with a layer of wax, written on with a sharp, pointed instrument called a stylus. Students often attended up to three lectures a day. They had a break for dinner in the late morning and then returned for more lectures in the afternoon. Then they were expected to return home to their rooms to spend the evening studying notes and books. Usually, students went to bed by eight or nine o'clock. After four or five years of liberal arts studies, a student received a degree and then could get a license as a teacher or continue studying to get a degree in theology, law, or medicine.

Not Always So Devoted

Most students were serious and studious, but many also spent a lot of time having fun. They drank in taverns and alehouses, played sports, gambled, and generally had a good time instead of studying. One French father wrote complainingly to his son, "I have recently discovered that you live dissolutely and slothfully, preferring license to restraint and play to work and strumming a guitar while the others are at their studies, whence it happens that you have read but one volume of law while your more industrious companions have read several. Wherefore I have decided to exhort you herewith to repent utterly of your dissolute and careless ways, that you may no longer be called a waster and your shame may be turned to good repute."[54]

In Paris, the self-indulgent, fun-seeking students sang a little song about themselves that goes:

"Time passes on
And nothing I've done;
Time is repeated,
And nothing I do."[55]

Medieval Scholars: Philosophy and Literature

All universities had their share of slackers, but medieval universities also produced influential and distinguished thinkers, writers, and philosophers who contributed to the progression of society and humanity. Petrarch, for instance, studied law but he discovered that he disliked the subject and found himself drawn to the studies of the classical literature and poetry of ancient Rome. Petrarch became a poet and literary scholar instead of a lawyer. He believed that Christian doctrine was not the only truth available to people and that classical literature was a worthwhile study. Both areas of philosophy, he thought, could help people grow and understand themselves. Petrarch was the world's first humanist. Humanism is a philosophy based on the idea that human beings, their thoughts, and the rational evidence they acquire from the world are more valuable and meaningful than pure faith or memorized religious doctrine. Petrarch was not antireligious in his humanism. He had become a member of the clergy, and he held that both ways of thinking were valid. He was deeply religious, but medieval society sometimes disapproved of his subject matter. Instead of writing poems about God, Petrarch wrote love

Petrarch, a medieval poet and scholar, followed the humanist philosophy. Humanism stresses the potential value and goodness of human beings, emphasizes common human needs, and seeks rational ways of solving human problems.

sonnets. He wrote about the beauty of nature and the universal pain of human emotional struggles. Petrarch argues, "In truth, poetry is not in the least contrary to theology. Does this astonish you? I might almost say that theology is the poetry of God."[56]

Thomas Aquinas, who studied at the University of Paris, was another famous man who joined the clergy but was also a scholar. He believed that reason was given to people by God and that reason, not just faith alone, was a path to God. In the late thirteenth century he wrote his masterwork *Summa Theologica* (Summary of Theology), which contained five logical proofs of the existence of God. Aquinas believed that theology should combine science and philosophy and that religion could be analyzed and proved true without relying solely on Church doctrine. His writings were sometimes criticized by the Church during his lifetime, but he was declared a saint in 1323, and since that time his doctrines have been an admired and accepted part of Christian religious thought. Pope John Paul II said that "the Church has been justified in consistently proposing St. Thomas as a master of thought and a model of the right way to do theology."[57]

Perhaps the most famous of medieval writers was Dante Alighieri, whose greatest work is *The Divine Comedy*. Dante studied philosophy at the universities in Bologna and Padua. He was not a member of the clergy, but his book is about the afterlife—Hell, Purgatory, and Heaven, and the sins for which people suffer after death. The modern poet W.B. Yeats called Dante "the chief imagination of Christendom,"[58] but during his lifetime, Dante got in some trouble for his imagination and his political views. He got into a feud with Pope Boniface VIII, who had imprisoned the former pope, Celestine V, to consolidate his own power, especially in Italian cities. Celestine had resigned, and some, including Dante, bitterly believed the abdication was due to pressure from Boniface. Boniface declared that popes were absolute rulers—not only over the Church but also over governments and cities. Dante wrote against papal control in his hometown of Florence and against the pope. Florence's government was on Boniface's side and punished Dante with banishment. In his book, Dante describes a character (unnamed, but obviously Boniface) who had sinned by committing religious fraud and is now hanging upside down

Looking Back

A Medieval Joke

During medieval times people enjoyed a good joke as much as they do today. One such story was told during the thirteenth century about some fun-loving students at the University of Paris and a well-fed cat belonging to their boardinghouse's owner. Historian Morris Bishop tells the joke this way:

> Some students were frequented in their lodging by a friendly cat. "He eats here free," they said; "make him join in the dice game." They contrived to make him roll the dice; he lost. They then tied a bill for a quart of wine to his neck and sent him home. The owner returned him with the money and a message: "Don't let him shoot dice anymore. He can't count good."

Morris Bishop, *The Middle Ages*. New York: American Heritage, 1970, p. 270.

in Hell with fire raining down on his feet. Dante was permanently exiled from Florence, sentenced to being burned at the stake if he returned.

Medieval Science

Being both a philosopher and a political activist could be dangerous during medieval times. Even scientists sometimes needed courage. Medieval science was primitive and based on logic and debate instead of scientific discovery. The thirteenth century philosopher and scientist Roger Bacon was one of the first in Europe to argue that science and knowledge should be based on research, observation, and experimentation. Bacon was educated at Oxford and also joined the clergy. He became a friar and a professor at Oxford, where he made many enemies by attacking other professors as ignorant. Bacon rejected blind faith and sheepish following of tradition. He argues, "Experimental science is the queen of sciences and the goal of all speculation."[59]

Some educated men refused to learn any other language except Latin. Bacon advocated learning Greek so as to be able to understand ancient Greek scientists. He studied Arabic writers, who were much more scientifically advanced than Europeans. For a while Bacon was supported by Pope Clement IV in his writings about the scientific method, but when the pope died, Bacon lost the Church's approval. He was imprisoned at a convent in Ancona, Italy, for his controversial ideas about theological reform and understanding the world through science instead of faith. The charge was listed as "suspected novelties" in teaching. Historians believe that Bacon spent about twelve years in confinement. Some of Bacon's novel ideas included the belief that the Earth was a sphere, not flat; a prediction of the invention of telescopes; and a mathematical effort to determine the distance to the stars. It was Bacon who famously said, "A little learning is a dangerous thing but none at all is fatal."[60]

> **WORDS IN CONTEXT**
> **alchemy**
> The medieval chemical science and philosophy that sought to transmute common metals into gold and also produce a universal cure for disease by means of the philosopher's stone.

Bacon was a brilliant man for his time, but like most of the medieval philosophers and scholars, he believed in astrology and alchemy. Alchemy is the theory that all matter is composed of various mixtures of basic elements and that the purest mixture—gold—could be derived from other matter if the scientist could discover a fifth element that would make gold out of any other metal. This fifth element was called the philosopher's stone. Of course, such an element does not exist, but the philosophers and scientists who searched for it represented the beginnings of modern chemistry. Albertus Magnus, a friar, scholar, and the teacher of Thomas Aquinas, was an alchemist who spent years searching for the philosopher's stone. A legend about him as a magician has been told for centuries: He actually discovered the philosopher's stone but never used it. Then, on his deathbed, he bequeathed the secret to St. Thomas, who destroyed it so that its power could never do any harm. The story is not true (Thomas Aquinas died before Albertus did), but Albertus Magnus did discover chemical elements and did believe that alchemy was a true science. In his writings he says that he had seen gold created by alchemy, although he never claimed that he had discovered the philosopher's stone.

Astrology was another area of scientific inquiry pursued by Albertus and many other scientists and philosophers. Albertus wrote a book, *Speculum Astronomiae*, which means Mirror of Astronomy. Astrology, for Albertus, was "the science of the judgments of the stars."[61] To medieval scholars, it seemed perfectly reasonable to believe that the power of the stars and planets affected what happened on Earth. The Christian philosophy was that God had created the universe for humans, and Earth was the center of the universe. A human being was a small world that functioned in the larger world of the universe, influenced by the movements and patterns of sun, moon, stars, and planets. Heavenly bodies affected—and could be used to predict—Earth's tides, floods, earthquakes, and other natural disasters, and they influenced human actions, as well. To men like Albertus Magnus and Thomas Aquinas, the philosophy of astrology fit with the idea of God's absolute power, but it did not mean that people did not have free will. The Heavens might influence emotions or personality traits, but people determined their own futures. Aquinas writes that anyone could choose to resist his "passions" and explains, "Wherefore the astrologers themselves are wont to say that 'the wise man is stronger than the stars.'"[62]

Medieval Medicine

Astrology was an integral part of medical science, too, because medieval physicians believed that the heavens controlled the elements of the human body just as they influenced the tides of the oceans. Astrology often told the doctor which treatment to try or which to avoid because the "signs" were wrong. Nevertheless, during the high Middle Ages in Italy, physicians began to move away from speculation about God and the universe and to use a practical approach to treating patients. Trained physicians tried to

An unfortunate patient endures the pain of having a badly healed leg fracture rebroken by a doctor. Medieval doctors knew little about the human body and had no knowledge of germs, but some tried to base their treatments on practical experience.

base their treatments on as much scientific information as was available at the time.

The first western European medical school was established in Salerno, Italy, during the tenth or eleventh century. A large hospital was attached to the medical school. Other early Italian universities with medical programs were at Bologna and Montpellier. At the Italian universities and hospitals physicians were interested in learning to treat medical problems, not in discussing the astrology of disease or the religious reasons for it. They performed dissections in order to understand the body; they treated wounds, practiced cleanliness (even with no knowledge of germs), and set broken bones; they tried to treat fevers and other illnesses in practical ways and attempted to diagnose illness and its prognosis (eventual outcome) scientifically, through observation and examination. To be certified as a physician, students had to first spend at least three years acquiring a general liberal arts university education, then study medicine for four years, and finally work under a qualified physician before they could practice medicine on their own.

At Salerno, women were allowed to train as physicians. The most famous was Trotula—the world's first gynecologist. Trotula specialized in women's health issues, wrote medical texts about women's health, and taught medicine at the University of Salerno. She was an expert in childbirth and taught about conception, pregnancy, delivery, and even how to sew up a patient who suffered tears during the birth process. She gave her patients drugs from plants to ease the pain of childbirth, even though the Christian belief was that women ought to suffer during childbirth, as Eve did in the Bible.

Surgery as a medical specialty advanced remarkably during the high Middle Ages. In the thirteenth century at the University of Bologna, William of Saliceto was instrumental in laying the foundations of modern surgery. He wrote and taught about diagnosis, sterile surgical procedures, suturing battlefield wounds, and using a knife for surgically removing dead tissue and growths. Before William's time, surgery was not considered medicine; it was performed by barbers since doctors thought surgery beneath them. Doctors believed that signs of infection like pus were good for healing, and they burned tissue rather than cutting it. One of William's students, Guido Lanfranchi, brought surgical knowledge to

> **WORDS IN CONTEXT**
> **astrology**
> The study of the heavenly bodies and their movements in order to determine their influence on Earth and on human affairs.

France and is considered to be the father of French surgery. Lanfranchi insisted that "no one can be a good physician who has no idea of surgical operations, and that a surgeon is nothing if ignorant of medicine."[63]

Moving Toward an Enlightened Age

The physicians and scientists of medieval times knew nothing of cells, microbes, or the true causes of disease. They had no modern instruments—not even thermometers or microscopes. Nevertheless, the best of them were enlightened and thoughtful people who helped both science and culture make a great leap forward during the high Middle Ages. During the late Middle Ages, when plague, famine, renewed warfare, and population devastation came to Europe, some of the knowledge was forgotten for a while, but the books and teachings survived through the dark times. The progress made during the high Middle Ages helped civilization recover and move forward into the modern era.

Source Notes

Introduction: The High Middle Ages

1. C. Warren Hollister, *Medieval Europe: A Short History*, 5th ed. New York: Wiley, 1982, p. 2.
2. Frances Gies and Joseph Gies, *Life in a Medieval Village*. New York: Harper & Row, 1990, p. 17.

Chapter One: Castle Life

3. Morris Bishop, *The Middle Ages*. New York: American Heritage, 1970, p. 88.
4. Quoted in Dominique Barthelemy, "Civilizing the Fortress: Eleventh to Thirteenth Century," in Philippe Aries and Georges Duby, ed., *A History of Private Life: Vol. II: Revelations of the Medieval World*, trans. Arthur Goldhammer. Cambridge, MA: Belknap Press of Harvard University Press, 1988, p. 406.
5. Bishop, *The Middle Ages*, p. 129.
6. Quoted in Gies and Gies, *Life in a Medieval Village*, p. 175.
7. Quoted in Bishop, *The Middle Ages*, p. 139.
8. Quoted in Hollister, *Medieval Europe: A Short History*, p. 162.
9. Bishop, *The Middle Ages*, p. 143.
10. Quoted in John Henry Parker, *Some Account of Domestic Architecture in England from Edward I to Richard II, with Notices of Foreign Examples and Numerous Illustrations of Existing Remains from Original Drawings*. Oxford: J.H. Parker, 1882, p. 72. http://books.google.com.
11. Bishop, *The Middle Ages*, p. 148.
12. Quoted in Emily Gosden, "Chivalry Explained: From Knights of Honour to Women's Lib," *Telegraph (UK)*, June 15, 2011. www.telegraph.co.uk.
13. Quoted in David R. Shumway, *Modern Love: Romance, Intimacy, and the Marriage Crisis*. New York: NYU Press, 2003, p. 14.

14. Quoted in Hollister, *Medieval Europe: A Short History*, p. 168.

15. Quoted in Philippe Braunstein, "Toward Intimacy: The Fourteenth and Fifteenth Centuries," in Aries and Duby, eds., *A History of Private Life*, p. 616.

Chapter Two: Village Life

16. Gies and Gies, *Life in a Medieval Village*, pp. 31, 33.

17. Gies and Gies, *Life in a Medieval Village*, p. 34.

18. Quoted in Gies and Gies, *Life in a Medieval Village*, p. 114.

19. Eleanor Searle, "Women and Marriage in Medieval Society," California Institute of Technology Library, April 1981, p. 19. http://calteches .library.caltech.edu.

20. Bishop, *The Middle Ages*, p. 242.

21. Quoted in Bishop, *The Middle Ages*, p. 243.

22. Quoted in Wally Seccombe, *A Millennium of Family Change: Feudalism to Capitalism in North Western Europe.* New York: Verso, 1995, p. 151.

23. Quoted in *Journal of the Statistical Society of London,* vol. VIII, *Statistical Society of London.* London: John William Parker, 1845, p. 160. http://books.google.com.

24. Barbara A. Hanawalt, "Narratives of a Nurturing Culture: Parents and Neighbors in Medieval England," *Essays in Medieval Studies*, vol. 12, in Nicole Clifton and J. Frantzen, eds., Illinois Medieval Association. www.illinoismedieval.org.

25. Quoted in Gies and Gies, *Life in a Medieval Village*, p. 137.

26. Jane Gilbert, "A Medieval Christmas," Time Travel–Britain.com, 2005. www.timetravel-britain.com.

27. Quoted in Fritz Rorig, *The Medieval Town.* Berkeley: University of California Press, 1969, p. 27.

Chapter Three: City Life

28. Quoted in Jean Manco, "Researching Historic Buildings in the British Isles," July 26, 2008. www.buildinghistory.org.

29. Hollister, *Medieval Europe: A Short History*, p. 158.

30. Quoted in Hollister, *Medieval Europe: A Short History*, p. 158.

31. Bishop, *The Middle Ages*, p. 210.

32. William R. Enger "Medieval Civilization I," Study Guide, Trinity Valley Community College, Athens, Texas. www.tvcc.edu.

33. Quoted in Robert Cole, *A Traveller's History of Paris*. New York: Interlink, 2003, p. 52.

34. Bishop, *The Middle Ages*, p. 248.

35. Quoted in Stephen Alsford, "Introduction: A Description of London," Florilegeum Urbanum. http://users.trytel.com.

36. Bishop, *The Middle Ages*, p. 258.

37. Quoted in Alsford, "Introduction: A Description of London."

38. Krystal Morgan, "Handspinners of the Later Middle Ages and Renaissance, Damask Weaver." http://damaskweaver.files.wordpress.com.

39. Bishop, *The Middle Ages*, p. 251.

Chapter Four: Religious Life

40. Christopher Holdsworth, "A Cistercian Monastery and Its Neighbours," *History Today*, vol. 30, no. 8, August 1980. www.history today.com.

41. Quoted in Clio Project, "Religious Nuns of Medieval Europe: Women of Action," Clio Project.org, p. 4. www.clioproject.org.

42. Quoted in Clio Project, "Religious Nuns of Medieval Europe," p. 3.

43. Hollister, *Medieval Europe: A Short History*, pp. 196–97.

44. Quoted in Hugh O'Reilly, "Urban II Calls for the First Crusade," World History, Tradition in Action, April 18, 2008. www.tradition inaction.org.

45. Fulcher of Chartres, *"The Chronicle of Fulcher of Chartres,"* in Peter Edwards, ed., *The First Crusade: "The Chronicle of Fulcher of Chartres"and Other Source Materials*, 1st ed. Philadelphia: University of Pennsylvania Press, 1998, p. 255.

46. Quoted in United Methodist Women, The Bible: The Book That Bridges the Millennia, "The Christian Crusades, 1095–1291," United Methodist Women. http://gbgm-umc.org.

47. The Aquinas Site, "The Sanctity and Miracles of St. Thomas Aquinas from the First Canonisation Enquiry." http://sedevacantist.com.

48. Bishop, *The Middle Ages*, p. 159.

49. Quoted in Gies and Gies, *Life in a Medieval Village*, p. 168.

50. Ellen N. La Motte, "The Hôtel-Dieu of Paris—An Historical Sketch," *Medical Library and Historical Journal*, vol. 4, no. 3, September, 1906, pp. 225–26. www.ncbi.nlm.nih.gov.

Chapter Five: Life of Learning

51. Oliver Weis, "The 7 Liberal Arts—Trivium, Quadrivium and Logical Fallacies," Matrixwissen.de. www.matrixwissen.de.

52. Isabelle de Foix, "A Tale of Two Medieval Universities: Bologna and Paris," Tripod.com. http://scholar76.tripod.com.

53. Quoted in Charles H. Haskins, "The Life of Medieval Students as Illustrated by Their Letters," *American Historical Review*, vol. III: October 1897–July 1898. New York: MacMillan, 1898, p. 210. http://archive.org.

54. Quoted in Haskins, "The Life of Medieval Students as Illustrated by Their Letters," p. 214.

55. Quoted in Bishop, *The Middle Ages*, p. 270.

56. Quoted in Marjorie O'Rourke Boyle, *Petrarch's Genius: Pentimento and Prophecy.* Berkeley: University of California Press, 1991, p. 13. http://ark.cdlib.org.

57. Quoted in Pope Benedict XVI, "Saint Thomas Aquinas—Part 1," Dominicans Interactive, June, 2010. www.dominicansinteractive .com.

58. Quoted in James E. Kiefer, "Dante Alighieri, Poet, Spiritual Writer," Biographical Sketches of Memorable Christians of the Past, Society of Archbishop Justus. http://justus.anglican.org.

59. Quoted in J.J. O'Connor and E.F. Robertson, "Roger Bacon," School of Mathematics and Statistics, University of St. Andrews Scotland, 2003. www-history.mcs.st-and.ac.uk.

60. Quoted in J.J. O'Connor and E.F. Robertson, "Roger Bacon."

61. Quoted in Gordon Fisher, *Marriage and Divorce of Astronomy and Astrology: A History of Astral Prediction from Antiquity to Newton.* Raleigh, NC: Lulu.Com, 2006, p. 166.

62. Quoted in John Scott Lucas, *Astrology and Numerology in Medieval and Early Modern Catalonia*. Leiden, Netherlands/Boston, MA: Brill, 2003, p. 12.

63. Quoted in Henry Ebenezer Handerson, *Gilbertus Anglicus, Medicine of the Thirteenth Century*. Cleveland, OH: Cleveland Medical Library Association, 1918, p. 77. http://books.google.com.

For Further Research

Books

Kathy Allen, *The Horrible, Miserable Middle Ages*. North Mankato, MN: Capstone, 2011.

Constance Brittain Bouchard, *Knights in History and Legend*. Buffalo, NY: Firefly, 2009.

Don Nardo, *Medieval Europe*. Greensboro, NC: Morgan Reynolds, 2011.

Don Nardo, *Medieval European Art and Architecture*. Detroit: Lucent, 2012.

Michael Riley and Jamie Byrom, *The Crusades: Conflict and Controversy, 1095–1201*. London: Hodder Education, 2013.

Adam Woog, *The Early Middle Ages*. San Diego, ReferencePoint, 2012.

Adam Woog, *The Late Middle Ages*. San Diego, ReferencePoint, 2012.

Websites

Castles of Britain (www.castles-of-britain.com/index.htm). This huge website, assembled by historian and castle enthusiast Lisa Hull, describes everything anyone could wish to know about the castles of the United Kingdom. Click "Castle Links" at the bottom of the Home page to find information, photos, and drawings about specific British castles.

Francesco Petrarch & Laura DeNoves (http://petrarch.petersadlon .com). This entire website, created by Peter Sadion in admiration of Petrarch, is devoted to the poet and to Laura, the love of his life. It includes pictures, writings, biographies, quotes, and music set to Petrarch's poems.

The Knight with the Lion (www.abdn.ac.uk/english/lion/index.shtml). This imaginative, interactive site tells stories of King Arthur and his knights, while including factual information about the time period and the people. It also provides audio demonstrations of medieval music and readings of old French writings.

Life in the Middle Ages (www.middle-ages.org.uk/life-in-middle-ages .htm). This extensive website explores the life of many kinds and classes of people during medieval times, as well as covering specific topics such as clothing, food, and entertainment.

Medieval Life and Times (www.medieval-life-and-times.info/index.htm). Visitors can click links to learn about such topics as religion, castle life, art, tortures, knights, women, and music at this large website. There is even a section about famous people from medieval times.

Medieval-Life.net (www.medieval-life.net/life_main.htm). Not only daily life but also the medieval histories of many different countries are included in this website.

Index

Note: Boldface page numbers indicate illustrations.

Picture Credits

About the Author

Toney Allman holds degrees from Ohio State University and the University of Hawaii. She currently lives in Virginia, where she enjoys a rural lifestyle, as well as researching and writing about a variety of topics for students.